YOUR LIFE AS A MOVIE

Scripting and Producing Your Dreams Into Reality

Edited by Sid Tafler

ISBN-13: 978-1507595848
ISBN-10: 1507595840

www.yourlifeasamovie.ca

To Dozer

You were by my side for every page of this book.

You reminded me when to work, when to eat,

and when to go for a walk.

Thank you for waiting until I finished before leaving.

CONTENTS

"IF I WON'T BE MYSELF, WHO WILL?"

Alfred Hitchcock

PREFACE

There have been events in my life that have been out of my control. I have always accepted them as they came and never questioned whether I played any part in these occurrences.

That was until I met Bob Proctor. I had heard about Bob over the past 20 years through various management training seminars I had attended, books I had read, and webinars that I had seen. He is known as the "master thinker" spending the last 50 years studying human growth, habits and potential.

He had always been sending the same message. "Tell me what you want and I'll show you how to get it."

I often wondered what type of person would make such a statement unless he believed in it completely. After all that is a pretty tall order to promise people. I believed life was happening to me, but Bob felt it was happening through me and that I could control the outcome.

My skepticism didn't come overnight. Like many people, I would get involved in some type of seminar or book, I would be on a high for about a week or so, deciding I was going to change my life and reach for amazing things, only to find that within a couple of weeks' time, I was right back to my original self, in my comfort zone with no changes.

Listening to Bob one day he had mentioned that it was all right for me to be skeptical but to just once, do what he was saying and prove him wrong. Being a bit of a competitive person, I took him up on the challenge. I had no right to assume he was not telling the truth about what he was teaching. I should do what he was saying and see if I got the results I expected and then I could be done with it once and for all. I could prove that he was just another motivational speaker on the circuit. I had heard the message before that what I think about comes about, but to be able to use it to get whatever I wanted was a bit over the top. I mean really, how can a thought control what I will attract in my life? This was going to be easy.

So, I did exactly what Bob told me to do to get anything I wanted. I read everything to the letter, not just once but many times to make sure I understood it all completely. I took every step he told me to do, exactly the way he said. When I was done and I felt I was ready, I ventured out to get what I wanted. Being the cautious person that I am, I decided to start small.

I wanted a cup of coffee.

You see, I am a coffee fanatic. I love everything about coffee. If there is one thing that will cheer me up, motivate me, or give me a boost it is my coffee. Nothing fancy, a non-fat latte is perfect. To me it defines comfort.

At the time I was working full time, nine to five in an office in Vancouver. It had a coffee shop nearby where a couple of times a week I would buy myself a latte as a treat. The rest of the days I would bring my coffee from home in my thermos.

My goal was that I wanted a tall non-fat latte delivered to me at my desk, without me having to go out to get it. I didn't know how it was going to happen. I just knew that it was my order and Bob promised me if I did everything he told me to, I would get my coffee. I created a perfect image in my mind of my having a cup of coffee delivered to me at my desk.

Now I'm sure this sounds trivial at this point. Most people would wish for a million dollars, however at the time, I did not believe that a million dollars was obtainable, but I believed I might be able to get a coffee. I mean all I had to do was ask someone going to the coffee shop to pick me up a coffee and my request would happen, right?

But I wanted to do this right, so I kept my project to myself and waited.

A couple of days into my experiment I remember arriving at work and sitting at my desk feeling quite tired. It was a cold damp day, pouring rain, I had just been driving for an hour in traffic, and my office was freezing.

With my back to the door, I gazed out my window at my car in the parking lot and was wondering what it would be like if I just got right back in my car and drove home. I wondered if this was the life I was destined to live, working in a cold office, alone and at my desk eight hours a day pushing papers. I thought about Bob and his teachings and tried to keep my spirits up.

I just wanted that coffee.

Suddenly, I heard footsteps behind me. I was a bit startled just to have someone arriving as I was always an hour ahead of anyone else in the office.

As I began to swing around to see who it was, an arm came around from behind and placed something in front of me on my desk. I realized the arm was that of a co-worker of mine, a man who had been with our office for a few weeks. I was surprised and relieved to see it was him. I then looked at what was placed in front of me.

It was a tall, non-fat latte.

I remember I was just staring at the coffee as he told me how he happened to be thinking of me driving in this awful weather and thought it would be a nice gesture to have my favourite coffee waiting for me. He then went on to say that he was upset I got there before him because he wanted it to be a surprise on my desk when I came in.

I often wonder how I would have reacted should I have come into an empty room with my coffee sitting there.

This is a silly story, right? You bet. I was the first to say this was a coincidence.

But then it started happening all around me. People from down the hall suddenly would pop their heads into my office asking if I wanted a coffee.

People bought me coffees for no apparent reason. In the year I had been there no one gave me a coffee and now the coffees were coming. Odd? Yes, but it was still just a coincidence in my mind. Perhaps I had inadvertently hinted for someone to buy me a coffee. Maybe I was complaining that I needed a coffee and someone heard me. I don't know. I just know that I didn't totally agree that I had made it happen. I knew there had to be an explanation.

So I decided to go bigger. I started asking for bigger and better things. I did my experiments one at a time, focusing on one thing that I wanted, either at work or in my home life. Little by little, they came to me, just as I would order them. As long as I did everything Bob told me to do, it happened. People that wouldn't give me the time of day in the past were now lunching with me. Money would come to me in different scenarios, I received things from the most unexpected places and I would achieve things I never thought possible. I got a new car, a new house, a bigger salary. The time that it took for the deliveries varied but if I just waited and believed they would come, they did.

And to think it all started with a coffee. For me, Bob Proctor is larger than life and I am blessed to know him. He has been delivering his message for over 50 years in fact, he started in 1961, the year I was born. The difference with me was that I was finally open to hearing his message. Until you are ready to receive something it doesn't matter how many times it is given to you, you will not accept it. You have to be ready to receive the message and I guess I was ready.

It all starts with an idea, a thought, and then learning how to develop it.

Aside from spending time with my family, my favorite pastime is the movie business. I love to learn about the making of movies, how they are put together, the way the story is told and how it is captured on the screen for us to enjoy. So it goes without saying that when I wanted to pass on what I learned from Bob I would use that particular medium. The parallel in your having a vision and obtaining it and that of coming up with an idea for a movie and producing it, are identical.

To obtain anything you want you have to first learn to use your imagination. Just like the idea for a movie, it all starts in your mind. All scripts are written by writers who take real life events or ideas from their imagination to create their story. There are some great messages intertwined in movie dialogue and I have shared some in this book to make some points. It is for that reason I am giving you a spoiler alert for the movies I mention in the book as I sometimes reveal the secrets to the plots involved.

I hope you enjoy the way this book takes you on a journey of discovery. It is divided into three parts. Lights: where you first look inwards to who you are now. Camera: where you are looking outwards to who you want to be. Action: where you discover how to have what you want.

My goal is to provide a format to follow, step by step, in order to get a clear picture in your mind for what you want in life.

If movies are an art, and art imitates life, then let's make your life a movie.

Francesca Banting

LIGHTS!

Illuminating the Mind

The Thoughts Within

CHAPTER 1

Movies and the Magic of Make Believe

Before we get started, I have one question for you. What are you looking for? That may seem like a loaded request but it is important that you know how to answer the question.

Is there one thing in your life that has always been at the back of your mind but for whatever reason you have not done or attained it? If you are like most people, you may say yes to this and answer with a career, a partner, money, health, happiness. These seem to be the stock answers.

I believe that most of us aren't really looking at all, but we are in fact *watching*. I think you should know the difference in the two words before you get started.

When you look for something it is very specific. You know what you want and you go out and find it. Looking for something has the expectation of obtaining it in the end because you are emotionally attached to it and want it. It originated from within yourself, and knowing that, you go outside yourself to find it.

If you don't find it, one of two things can happen. You may give up the search completely, accept that it is not attainable then convince yourself you could not find it. Sometimes this can be at a cost, either emotionally or financially. You settle for a different outcome than you expected and it may be with great disappointment or regret.

The second scenario is to step up the search, leave no stone unturned until you find what it is you are looking for, no matter the cost emotionally or financially. This process takes more time and energy but the reward is much more fulfilling. When you find what you were looking for, you experience a great feeling of excitement and accomplishment.

For example, what would happen if you lost your car keys? Those keys open the door to the vehicle that gets you where you want to go when you need to get there. Without them you are lost and your emotions are possibly triggered while you search. When you go to look for them, you know exactly what you're looking for; you may see other keys but you know to ignore those ones because they are not specific to your car. When you find them, there is that great relief, that wonderful euphoria of finding what you were looking for and achieving the result.

But what if you don't find them? You must search until you find the keys to get into your car. If you don't ever find them, you'll do anything it takes to find an alternative to get into that vehicle, usually by getting another set of keys made. There is no option but to find a way to get in and drive that car. It makes sense, right? It is the only logical thing to do. You would not go out and buy a new car, would you?

As crazy as it sounds, this is what many of us do with our dreams. We stop looking and settle for the next best thing, usually at an emotional cost, then regret that we never tried harder to look until we found it. At the first obstacle we stop looking and go for the alternative, settling for believing that what we are looking for cannot be found. We go out and buy another dream, an alternative, and live with the regret of not looking harder. We may carry the emotional pain with us forever.

We buy the new car, the new dream, instead of finding the keys. All we had to do was look harder. To avoid the pain of having to do this over again, we decide that dreams are too hard to look for so we find another way to live.

We stop looking and start watching.

When you watch, you see someone or something else doing or being something, but you are not participating. You can pretend to be involved in what they are doing, but you do not have to commit. You can take yourself out of the equation at any time. You can watch everything around you and choose when you will go along for the ride emotionally, and not be tied to the outcome because you are safely watching from the sidelines. There is no ownership to it.

Think about the last time you watched someone attempt to attain something. They may have known what they were looking for and decided to do things differently from what they had been watching others do for so long.

How many times did you take part in assessing their situation, judging them on their performance as they attempted to achieve their goals, sometimes laughing and making fun of them? You may have criticized them for doing something stupid or making a poor decision. But just as quickly as we can condemn, we can take part in their glory by celebrating with them when they achieve what they were searching for, especially when they are winners.

You have been watching others achieve their goals many times, yet you remained stuck, not knowing how to obtain what it is you wanted in life.

People who are achieving the goals that are making them happy have discovered to get what they want out of life is internal, not external. These individuals learned that "seeing is believing" but saw it in their minds first.

What you constantly see over and over again begins to be your reality whether seen externally or internally. If you are watching things externally, you will take that as fact and begin to believe it and keep that result. What you need to do is take control and see things internally to change the results externally.

If you are an overweight person who wants to lose weight, think about your bathroom scale. You keep looking at it regularly and it keeps telling you, "You are overweight." No matter how hard you try, you remain overweight. Until you understand that what you need to be looking at is internal to create the external, your results are always going to be the same. You regularly see that you are overweight, so what you see you believe, and you stay overweight.

If you can see yourself internally as being the weight you want to be, you would not rely on the things you see externally to tell you what weight you are. You would believe you are the weight you want to be and you would create the result from internal to external.

I don't know about you, but I would much rather watch the internal movie because it would make me feel good. And it is that feeling that you need to have to create your results.

Think about what you spend the majority of your time watching.

When we get absorbed watching certain things, it can trigger an emotion inside of us that we are not capable of obtaining ourselves. We rely on what we see to get us charged inside when really we should be the one taking control and flicking the switch ourselves. We escape our own reality, even for a brief time, for the chance to see what it would feel like to be doing something else. It is entertaining.

Think about movies. For a couple of hours we are taken away into a fantasy life and we become the people in that situation. We get caught up in their lives, feel their emotions and experience their world.

That feeling stays with us after the movie, sometimes for a few hours or even a few days depending on how deeply the emotions were felt. But then you go back to your everyday life, back to your old emotional level unless you find a way to keep that feeling. You may watch the movie again, wait in anticipation for the sequel or buy memorabilia so that you can be reminded of that movie over and over again. What you need to realize is that it is the feeling that makes you become what you are thinking about.

Just look at any child who has seen a great movie that inspires them. They become obsessed with it, wanting to see it again and again, and wanting anything and everything to do with that character. The movie triggers the feeling inside of them and they become what they are feeling.

Many years ago I had that experience with my son when he discovered the Teenage Mutant Ninja Turtles cartoon. The transformation began with turning his bedroom into a Ninja Turtle lair, complete with bed linens, curtains, wall stickers and of course pajamas. He wore Ninja Turtle t-shirts and hats and he ate on Ninja Turtle plates. He camped in a Ninja Turtle tent and slept in his Ninja Turtle sleeping bag. We had to tape every episode on TV so he could watch throughout the day and we had every toy or poster that was made at that time. When the movie came out we were there front and centre and my son was absolutely thrilled.

The experience my son felt at that time was interesting because he was so happy with how he was feeling, this happiness spilled over into the rest of the family. There was an excitement in the air and he passed this feeling onto his friends and family. You just wanted to be around him to get some of that energy. This is why parents love doing things for their kids. It's such a great energy that gets passed around, how can you not enjoy yourself being around someone that exerts such a happy feeling?

It's similar to a person who has great energy walking into a room. It is like they bring a ray of sunshine into the room and you just suddenly feel good. Do you ever wonder how that person got to be so happy that they are constantly walking with a spring in their step? You just want to be around them in the hopes that something rubs off on you. What they are feeling is coming from the inside out. They are not looking outward to obtain their results. They created them internally. They did it all by feeling.

My son felt like a hero when he was a Ninja Turtle. He naturally wanted to explore things and protect people from danger. He wanted to be a hero.

He was emotionally attached to an idea, it produced a feeling inside, and it is that feeling that brought out his results.

If you know what you are looking for, and watch what supports your dream, it can motivate you to take charge of your own life and move into a new direction. If watching something creates an emotion in us, and the emotion is what creates the result, why not take control of what we watch?

It's time to start watching an inspiring and exciting movie that will transform your life. The secret is to know how to make the movie in your mind so that you can watch it over and over again and be the star! You watch it when you want, where you want.

You may be thinking that you do not know how to start and you have no idea how to do this. Don't worry about anything at this point. The first thing you have to do is to decide that you are worthy to make your movie and you have something inside that needs to be released. We all can easily talk ourselves out of doing things so I need you to firstly talk yourself into doing this process. Who you are right now is where you are supposed to start.

Many movies depict the lost person trying to find their way in life. I remember a scene in the movie "Lost in Translation" where Bill Murray and Scarlett Johansson are sharing a drink at a hotel bar in Tokyo. They are two Americans brought together by circumstance, he at least three times her age, and both are suffering from insomnia. In their almost catatonic states they meet regularly and begin to open up to one another. Bill Murray's character is looking back at his life questioning why he is where he is, and Scarlett's character is perplexed about where she is in her life, where she is going, recently married and just graduated from university with a major in philosophy. She is wondering if everything she has been focusing on so far has been misdirected. Bill, in a wise reassuring way says to her, "Don't worry, I'm sure you will find the angles." The words seem to be encouraging to her as she begins to process what he said and how it applies to her personally.

I'm not sure what the screenwriter intended the meaning to be, but I know what I took away from it. Scarlett had studied something she felt strongly about, she just didn't know how to apply it to her life, and as a profession. She was now married to a man who was there in Tokyo for his job, a professional photographer, and she was tagging along. She seemed lost and confused as she went through her life with no purpose.

How many times have you looked at something you have done in the past, perhaps a job or schooling, a relationship or a trip, and thought it was all a waste of time?

Maybe if you really looked back on it and focused a little better, you could find that the angles and parts of every event formed the person you are today. Everything you experienced took you to a different level of understanding and shaped you into who you are right now. This is your starting point. No one else has had the same experiences as you have so no one can see things like you do. Know that you truly are "individual" in who you are.

Everything you have learned and done so far has taken you to this point. You were meant to start here.

Take Bill Murray's advice and find your angle.

As we go on this journey from where you are now to where you want to be in the future, you are going to stop watching what is outside you and begin looking inside you. The angles will begin to make sense.

It all starts in your mind.

CHAPTER 2

Introducing "You"

There are many things that we had to learn to live that we have received internally and externally.

When was the last time you felt the warmth of sunshine on your face? Was it while you were enjoying a leisurely walk with your dog, vacationing on a tropical beach, or just relaxing on your back porch with a cold drink after a long day? The sun is a magnificent thing. It provides us and every other living creature on this earth with the nutrients we need to flourish. Without the sun, life on this planet would end.

But the sun's powerful energy can cause much harm. It has the ability to heat up so quickly and strongly that it can damage or destroy anything in its path. The amazing thing is that as we have evolved, we have learned to adapt to the changes in temperature by protecting ourselves for survival.

How do you block the sun from harming you? Do you cover yourself with lotion to block its rays, do you shield yourself from it with your hands or do you hide for cover?

Aside from the heating and energy properties we receive from the sun, we also have the natural illumination it provides. Light is so important, even God named it as the first thing on his to-do list. It truly is the source that keeps us from darkness. The laws of nature are in control of when and where the sun sends us our light. But being the inventive humans we are we found a way to adapt.

In the 1870s there was a man in the U.S. who was obsessed with securing the power of light. He knew there had to be a better way to illuminate homes so that people would not have to live in the dark. That man was Thomas

Edison. He was so dedicated that he devoted his time and energy into finding a way to harness light. He eventually did that by developing the first commercially practical light bulb, a source strong enough to brighten any room.

This man was so focused on the power of light that he found a way to not only capture it but take control and release it when he wanted and how he wanted. We now have the ability to bring light into our lives in times and places we never thought possible, at our command whenever we need it!

Light is and always will be the medium for us to see things more clearly. It lets us see what is around us, puts our minds at ease that there are no awful things that are going to harm us. We sense that what is in the dark can hurt us, but if we can see it, we can protect ourselves from any danger.

Think about the last time you were driving down a dark winding road that had no streetlights. You probably slowed down and were nervous about the unknown in the dark ahead. What obstacle could be on the road or jump out at you at any time? Then you clicked on your high beams and they lit up the road for you. I'm sure you were at ease once you could see the road more clearly. How many times were you afraid of the dark as a child and the light from a little nightlight somehow protected you from the bogeyman?

Our minds are capable of making us believe that things are there, so we physically turn on the lights to show us that what we imagined really isn't there. It is a sense of relief knowing that the bad things that we envisioned in the dark of our minds go away once they are lit. We use the external light around us to ease our internal mind.

Most things revolve around light so if we are going to be looking inward we need to imagine the light inside our minds. When is the last time you lit up your mind?

You have learned how to protect yourself from the harmful rays of the sun by covering up and hiding from them. Have you done that with your mind as well? The sun has a lot of nutrients that every living thing needs to grow. For you to grow you must have light in your mind as well. For you to be able to change or deal with what is there you first need to see what is in the darkness. It's time to shine a light on what's inside before you create something new.

To create a movie, we need to see where we are going to make all this happen. We need to turn the lights on so we can see what we are doing.

When you look at a movie being made, the location is mainly made up of cables and cords that extend up and over and through the set. It is littered with small, medium and large lights all pointing to specific things to ensure there is just the right lighting for the action in that particular scene.

A set can be built indoors to mimic the actual outdoors and it is the lighting that makes this happen. In the movie industry there are baby spots to light up small corners and the giant spotlights to illuminate larger sets.

These studio lights are designed with small shutter panels on the sides that can be opened and closed to control the direction of the light with precision. They can also be covered with filters to change the colour or soften the strength of the light emitted.

Because this movie we are creating is about you, I want you to focus now on that baby spot as if it was directed right at you. Now let's close those shutters a bit so the light is going directly into your mind. We want to look at the preview of coming attractions and to do that you are going to have to let the light enter. Let's install some baby spotlights in your mind and see what is there.

How you currently see things can be changed and to take control you need to allow your mind to be open to change. If you cannot let light, the source of energy into your mind, it will not grow. It will just stay in the darkness that it is now in.

As the baby spot is shining brightly on you, how do you feel about that? Is your first instinct to cover your eyes from the bright light and shy away from looking inwards? Perhaps there are some things you don't want to see as they are better left in the dark and you like to leave them undisturbed. Maybe you have just found a way to let the light in but you protect yourself from certain things by putting filters on the light.

The reasons we choose not to change and the excuses we use are endless. You need to know how important it is to be able to decide that you need to know who you are before you can change. Who you are now is a result of your past and the more you understand how you think the easier it will be to create your new movie.

Many of us go through life with the one view of life as we see it, never taking a chance to look for a possibility that there are other choices out there. We accept that how we see the world in our mind is how it really is.

Characters have been written to portray how individuals can be trapped in life when they have a closed mind. One movie that takes this concept to the extreme is the movie "Overboard" where Goldie Hawn plays an eccentric millionaire in a loveless marriage. She believes herself to be better than everyone because she is rich and has status and therefore treats her "help" in the most demeaning way. Her yacht is passing near a remote small town, it breaks down and she is forced to stay on her ship for a few days while it is being repaired. Kurt Russell plays a down and out widower and carpenter who is working day and night trying to support his four sons. He is hired to build a closet for the bored Hawn, and is constantly subjected to her insults and criticism. The story unfolds when Hawn's character, not satisfied with the work Russell provides, refuses to pay him for the job and threatens his livelihood by tossing his tools overboard. Russell is devastated and revengeful.

In a funny twist of events, Goldie's character falls off her boat, bangs her head on a garbage scow and ends up in the local hospital with amnesia. Russell, seeing an opportunity for "payback" scoops her from the hospital claiming she is his wife, and immediately puts her to work in his hovel of a home to care for him and his four sons.

The core of this movie becomes quite wonderful when Hawn becomes a loving and doting mother to the children and eventually falls in love with Russell. The old eccentric, spoiled rich girl is true to herself and is living happily ever after, in love and having the family she always wanted.

Eventually, she regains her memory and retreats back to her wealthy, unhappy life but as a more caring and thoughtful person, especially to her staff. Her rich family, appalled at how she had been living the past few months, are shocked to see her new demeanor and put her under psychiatric care. In their minds, her new behaviour is proof that she is crazy.

The integral part of this movie is when Hawn's butler confronts her about her return and her new-found personality. He, along with the rest of the staff, is enjoying their new friendly boss and is having a heart-to-heart conversation about her behaviour.

She apologizes to her butler for treating him so poorly in the past, and asks him if he thinks she is crazy like her family says because she's not the person she once was.

He replies with intense sincerity, "No Madame, oh no! Most of us go through life with blinders on Madame, knowing only that one little station to which we are born. You Madame, on the other hand, have had the rare privilege of escaping your bonds for just a spell. It's life from an entirely new perspective. How you choose to use that information is entirely up to you!"

This message from the butler pretty much sums up exactly what we all need to do. We need to understand that there are different versions of how we see things and we need to be open to understanding that concept. Hawn discovered that true happiness was not achieved by having money but by being in love. Once she took off the filters and removed the blinders, she saw things more clearly. How she chose to use that information was now up to her.

We are all different personalities, some do everything they are told to do, and others are so skeptical they freeze and never take on anything new. How will you choose to use the information?

What I am asking of you is to take the blinders off for just a while and try seeing things with a different perspective. Stop looking away and allow the light to shine brightly in your mind. Just like a movie set, we can't achieve anything until we see everything clearly and we get the lighting just right.

Before you can make this movie you need to understand that you will be in the spotlight. You are the star! As we go inwards to your mind, just remember to keep the lights on. You will see more clearly as we move along.

Just like Edison, you are going to harness the light that is inside of you and release it so that it can shine brightly for all to see.

You may know what you want or who you want to become, but for many that dream is buried so deep you can't locate it. It may have changed over the years as you have changed. Here is something you can do to help find what you want. It is an exercise that needs to be done quickly and timed in five-minute intervals.

Take a sheet of paper and make three columns. Label each column as A, B and C. You will begin by filling in column A. Set your timer for five minutes and as quickly as you can, write down everything that comes to mind that you want to BE.

This column should indicate who you are inside, a characteristic, a state of being that you want to feel on a continual basis. Do you want to be loyal, giving, caring, or loving? What is it that you want to express? This is the starting point of understanding who you are. The key is to write what first comes to mind without thinking too much about it. When you are done go back to the list and circle the top three of what you want to BE.

In column B, write down the list of things you want to Do. This column should list the things you see yourself doing to achieve what you wrote in column A. If you saw yourself doing this action would it confirm your selection from column A?

For example, if in Column A you wanted to be giving, in column B you may be feeding the hungry, giving donations, or sharing some information. It should show how to express what is in column A. As you did with column A, this column is also timed and then your top three items selected.

Finally, in column C write down what it is you want to Have in life. What is it that you need to have as a person? This is the result of your doing the action in column B. For example, if in column A you wanted to be independent, in column B you saw yourself earning money as a nurse, and in column C you had your own car. You would be satisfying your need in being independent with earning a living and being able to come and go as you please. As with the other two columns, you time your responses and then select the top three.

You should have three items from each column. At this point you need to pick the top item from each column. You may find it challenging but when you look closely enough you may really know what you want but you are afraid to say it. Don't worry, this is all about you and no one will see or hear your decision.

You need to know that whatever you feel the most emotion about is the one you need to select.

When you have your top three items, one from each column, you can now begin to form a picture of who you are.

It is important to allow your imagination to run free and really be part of the vision in your mind. Play around with this exercise for a while until you come up with a vision in your mind of whom and what you want to be.

The only limits are the ones you impose on yourself. Outside influences may have put limits on you in the past, but in your mind there are none. Dare to dream. Only you know what makes you feel good.

Take off the blinders, turn up the lights and really take the time to see who you are. Every movie starts with a great idea and it's time to shine the light on yours.

Just like a seedling, if you do not give your thought light, it will die because it needs the sun's nourishment to grow. Put yourself in the spotlight and watch yourself grow!

CHAPTER 3

Quiet on the Mind Set

Every great movie idea deserves a great studio to create it and we all know where those can be found--Hollywood!

The first thing that comes to my mind is the monumental gates of the movie studios. These structures represent the entrance to a land where lives are changed by being part of a fantasy world where dreams are made. To pass these gates means entering a place where people and their ideas are gathered and then transformed into reality and the final product is spit back out through the gates for us to see. It truly is the magic of Hollywood.

Paramount, MGM, Universal. They all have enormous lots and thousands of employees that come together to form what they hope will be the next blockbuster hit of the year.

If they can create sensational movies on their studio lots, then you deserve your own studio where your idea can be turned into a hit as well.

Your mind is actually designed just like a studio lot. Let's look at what happens in a movie studio.

The movie industry is lucrative and competitive and each of these studios wants to protect their assets, including their ideas.

Every person and everything that is brought into that studio serves a purpose in the final outcome of the story idea. The focus in that studio is solely on creating, producing and releasing that film. Everyone knows what the outcome should be and they all know the part they need to play to make it happen.

To ensure that the focus is entirely on their production, studios put in place a system that protects them from unwanted visitors and lets them control who and what can take part in the venture. They keep their ideas and productions to themselves. To do that, they build a giant wall around their offices and studio lot with only one access--a giant gate. Once they have their structure in place, they install a powerful force that controls their entire production--the gatekeeper.

Any company focused on the growth of an idea or a plan knows the importance of a gatekeeper. The sole purpose of the gatekeeper is to only allow into the studio what is necessary to complete the movie. Anyone or anything that will disrupt the flow or energy put into that idea is refused entry. The gates need to only be opened to those who will benefit the achievement of the goal.

Can you imagine a movie studio with no one guarding the gate? Fans would flood the studio trying to find their favourite movie stars on the lot. Competitors could come and go and steal ideas and staff. Shareholders would visit and impose their ideas and change the plans again and again. Aspiring actors and their agents would barge into offices looking for acting opportunities. The lot would be full of chaos and frustration and the chances of a movie being made would be greatly diminished. If the movie ever were to be made, it would be drastically different than the original concept. It would be full of changes and influences from what others impressed on it or even worse, a bunch of mediocre movies would be made and released but never the hit that they wanted. There would only be chaos. Studios would never be able to see their movie completed. It would always just be an idea floating around while others played with it and made changes all the time. Without order, the movie could not be made.

The best studios have their vision that they work on privately in their studio lot, and they control what comes through the gate. If they put all their attention on the vision, eventually the movie is made and released through the movie theatres for all of us to see.

I love this visual because what I have just described is pretty much a description of your mind.

I personally had a problem with learning about the mind. I was always confused about the conscious and the subconscious mind, how they worked, and how I could control their functions. Like most people, I needed to have a visual. It wasn't until a few years ago when I made the correlation that I am about to share with you that I was really able to take control and produce results. I needed to put order in my mind before I could make any changes.

I made my mind a movie studio.

If we look at how you are structured in comparison to a studio producing a movie, your mind is where the movie is to be made and your body is how the movie is projected for all to see.

What you create in your mind will be released through your actions and in turn will produce your results. Therefore if you create a vision in your mind, if directed correctly, it will be released as a production through your body. The key is to stay focused on the movie in your mind until it is completed and released through your actions. Just like the studio gate, if you have your mind open for all to enter, you have chaos and you will not be able to give attention to your dream and help it grow. To do that you need to build your mind studio.

The mind has many components to it but to simplify things we are to divide it into two parts, the conscious mind and subconscious mind.

Your conscious mind is your gatekeeper. It is where everything comes to you in life. It is all brought to you by the things you see, hear, touch, smell, and taste. Everything that comes into your life is shown to you through your conscious mind. It is the command station of your body. It is the place where everything you need is initiated. You have complete control of anything and everything that comes to the gate. You can accept what comes, or you can reject it.

When you have your vision in place, the movie you want to make, all you have to do is send the order to your conscious mind with what you will need to make it happen. When you are very clear, your conscious mind will be on the lookout for everything you need to make it happen. It will also dismiss anybody or anything that is not in direct correlation to the achievement of your goal.

Just like the gatekeeper, it is responsible for keeping anything not associated with the movie out of the studio lot. To do this, your conscious mind has to be very clear on what it is you need.

Your subconscious mind is the part of the mind that basically has to deal with everything the conscious mind hands to it. It has no choice to accept or reject, it just does what it is told and processes it. The conscious mind sends the information to the subconscious mind, it processes it, and then it releases it through the body as an action. Your subconscious mind is the studio lot.

You can see that if you are not sending the information that is important for you to attain your goal your mind can be full of chaos. You need to filter the information coming from your conscious mind and take control of only things that will focus on your vision.

For example, if you consciously look at something scary, your conscious mind will send the image to your subconscious mind and it will accept it. It has to, it has no choice. The subconscious mind, being the studio that produces what your results are, will spit out the emotion of fear through your body. It could be in the form of a gasp, a scream or a jolt. Whatever you pass through your conscious mind, it has to go into the subconscious mind and be sent out as a reaction.

If we want to have a new vision where the result is that we feel good and are happy, then the messages from our conscious mind to our subconscious mind should be those that are positive. It would be in our best interest to only have thoughts and information from our conscious mind that would apply to our new vision of feeling good and being happy to ensure we produce our results.

If you want to stay focused on your new vision, you need to first control what your conscious mind has access to. The great thing about the conscious mind is that it can accept or reject anything given to it. Unlike the subconscious mind, the conscious mind does not have to take anything it doesn't want. It is the gatekeeper.

If the conscious mind brings information to our subconscious mind through our senses, then we need to control as much of the things we are seeing, hearing, touching, tasting and smelling.

I want you to think of your subconscious mind as everything on the inside of the gate. The entire lot, including the sound stage is considered to be your subconscious mind. Everything and anything that passes through that gate will be put into your movie. Any information, good or bad, that passes through that gate is accepted. Once something or someone passes through that gate, it is on the lot and it is in your movie. If a bad person or idea enters, there is no way to make it leave. There is no exit gate and that which entered is there for life. The only thing to do with it is to find a way to apply it to your movie or find a place for it to be stored away.

When you think about this, you can quickly see how you need to take control of what enters your subconscious mind, or in this case your studio lot. If you allow just anything to enter, it will add chaos and distract you from working on your vision.

It is crucial then to do what the movie studios do and build a wall around your subconscious mind. You want to protect your vision and you can start by keeping your idea to yourself. You do not want to take the chance of someone trying to change it and impose their ideas on you. This is your original. To keep it that way you must stay true to your vision.

You need to take control of your movie studio.

You will be deciding who and what is allowed into your movie studio to make your blockbuster hit. You will have full control of the list of people and things that are needed to bring this script into fruition.

You have made the decision to take control of your life to create your new movie script and understanding that you are in control of what passes your gate is very important. Take control of your senses.

Start looking around you right now and notice how things are currently entering your mind on a daily basis. What sense are you currently using to allow things into your subconscious mind that you see will not serve a purpose in the future? Think of the shows you watch on television, the people you associate with, the foods you eat. Are any of the things you are paying attention to contributing to the vision you want in the future?

You may want to become a more positive person, but find that you spend your day watching negative news programs. Perhaps you want to be healthier and in better shape but are eating unhealthy foods and leading a sedentary life. When you really take a close look you will see how much time and energy you spend on things that do not serve you.

If you are clear on your vision, and you know what you are looking for you should be able to start seeing the things you need to allow into your studio. Pay attention to what you are currently allowing into your subconscious mind that is either keeping you where you are or leading you towards your goal. When you take control of the gate you have control of your movie and you can work faster and smarter on completing it.

You are going to learn how to focus on your movie and only to allow the people and things that are going to make your movie come to life. It is this small change that is going to make the biggest impact on your life.

CHAPTER 4

Your Mind Vault

You should have a better understanding of the importance of how setting up your studio lot will help you achieve what you want out of life. The more careful you are about what you allow in your mind, the better your results. But the pressing question I am sure you have is, "What about what is already there?" If you are like most people, your gates have been open all of your life and you have now learned that what is in your mind is there for good. What does that mean towards the attainment of your new goal?

Who you are today is a result of what you have learned throughout your life. Think of yourself as a movie that you are currently projecting that is a culmination of everything that has already passed through your gates. You are an original production.

To know how to change who you are, or change your current movie, know that you are being, doing and having your past vision. You are a result from your past thinking. To understand how your past thoughts are creating your current actions we can compare our memory imprinted on our minds to be similar to making a movie on film.

Do you ever wonder where the term "silver screen" came from? Much like silver tarnishes when it's exposed to air, film has silver components imbedded in it so that when it is hit by light, it forms the image. A movie is a series of images taken in a sequence to form a moving picture that is projected on a screen for everyone to see, hence the term *silver screen*.

A critical problem with original film has always been storage. Film is very delicate and if not properly stored it can be damaged or disintegrate by exposure to the elements. Movie studios work hard at storing and preserving their finished products by keeping them in sealed cans in climate-controlled rooms. Currently there are people around the world who work tediously just to restore these films to ensure we can view them for years to come. They meticulously go through frame-by-frame and restore or recreate the images, sometimes even converting them from black and white to colour. These preserved movies can be shown in their original format, copied as is, or altered to whatever the studio chooses. They can be hidden and never shown or they can be constantly projected as reruns, it all depends on what the studio chooses to do with them.

Your mind, like a studio vault, is currently protecting all of your film.

You, much like the movie studios, have your own storage system, your memory. Memories, just like movies on film, are permanently imprinted, and then kept in our minds waiting for when we want to recall them. Your memories are stored away and in a controlled environment, however, each one may be in a different state. Some may have deteriorated with time and are faded, others you run regularly and are very clear, and some you just leave in the back and hope they will never return and just disintegrate.

The more often you run a memory or movie in your mind, the more it will play out in your life. When you run memories continuously they eventually take over and you become what you are thinking about.

You currently have your own vault and it is full of emotions and memories that are playing simultaneously. They are responsible for forming the habits and behaviours that you have accumulated through your life. This is who you are now. It is a vault full of every event in your life and everything you have seen, heard, felt, touched or tasted in your life and is projecting through your body emotionally as the person you are today.

Your beliefs, ideas, culture, and thoughts that you have accumulated throughout your life are compiled into one large vault in your mind that dictates how you think. Remember, the way we received information into our subconscious mind was through our senses. We heard things that were told to us, we saw things that were shown to us, we tasted things that were fed to us, we touched things that we reached out for, and we smelled things that were emitted in the air. The labels that are on each may vary according to how you received the memory.

You are probably wondering then, why is it that you have experienced different things throughout your life that have had no effect on you. That is because those things were not imprinted. Everything that you have formed as a habit was put there in one of two ways. The first is by a shock to your system. An emotional shock, whether good or bad, will more than likely stay with you. It is that occurrence that was so enormous that it made an impact so deep that it was automatically stored.

The second is to have something shown or given to you continuously until it becomes a learned behavior or habit. You had to be exposed to it over and over again before you took it on as an imprint. Think of a song on a radio that you heard repeatedly until eventually you knew all the words. It's very rare to learn all the words with one listen. When you had a test in school, how did you memorize the answers? It was probably by studying the questions over and over until they became learned. Thoughts and ideas will come and go but it is the ones that we repeat on a regular basis that make the stored film.

When you were a child you obviously had no control of your conscious mind as you could not think for yourself. Everything that went inside your subconscious mind was put there by someone else's control of your studio gate.

When you came into this world you were the vision in someone's mind. Their dream was to have a child and you played a part in their movie. Your parents fed you, clothed you, nurtured you and raised you the way they knew how. You were given and taught things based on someone else's life and how they wanted you to fit in their dream.

Your subconscious mind learned behaviours from these individuals and subsequently these behaviours became imbedded in you as a habit. You had many things instilled in you including culture, people and events. You accepted everything put in your mind by your parents, guardians, and teachers. The people around you were deciding what they thought you needed and they allowed those things into your mind and you had no choice but to accept them, good or bad. They told you and demonstrated for you the same things over again until you accepted them as truth. Until you were in control of your conscious mind, you had no choice.

The interesting thing is that we were all taught with the same senses through our conscious mind, by feeling, tasting, seeing, hearing and smelling things. We have all learned to eat, but what we tasted and what we believed was good was shown to us in different ways.

This didn't become apparent to me until I was at school and around other children. I remember seeing the different lunches that my fellow students were eating. I had only been exposed to the foods that my parents introduced me to, but once in school, I smelled and tasted new things I had never seen before. It was a whole new world for me. We also grew up with different habits, religions and views on how to see things. My concept of what clean meant was totally different from someone else's, based on how they were raised. The same is true for feelings. My concept of what love feels like varies from what others have experienced. It was all very confusing to see the differences but also very exciting. We all learned the same things but with different examples.

Take some time to think about the things you believe and why you believe them. Was it something you were told to believe or was it from your own experiences?

If you want to change something about yourself now, you have to take into account the way your subconscious mind is projecting your current movies. If you do not have your conscious mind deliver an order to your subconscious mind, it will just fill in the actions for you. If you do not take control, it will just play a rerun of what it believes to be true.

This is evident when you consider the things you do day by day without thinking. How many times have you had a day off but have gotten into your car to go shopping and you start driving the route to work? Or you're watching TV but somehow you're putting food in your mouth, chewing and swallowing without consciously thinking about it. You walk without thinking, you blink without thinking. You are just going through the motions. Your subconscious mind fills how you will act and react unless you reprogram it with a new thought or action. This is how habits are formed. To change a current habit, you must impress the new vision over and over again until it becomes a new habit. If you don't, the subconscious mind will put in the old rerun for you to fill the space.

Think about all the habits and characteristics you have that are just running on autopilot. Many of the things you are doing in your life, the way you react and handle things, are all based on your past imprints, your past movies that you have developed as a habit. You have tied the memory of each event in your life to a specific emotion and your body expresses it with or without your consent.

This explains why you feel and react to certain things and don't understand why. For example, when you smell cookies it may take you back to when you were a child and you went to grandma's house. You impressed in your subconscious mind the memory of that event with a smell. Whenever you smell cookies you remember grandma.

What about the smell of medical ointment? Perhaps this brings back memories of when you would fall down a lot and it would sting when you put the medicine on your cut. You may get nervous when you smell ointment because it takes you back to those memories. This can explain why so many people do not like the smell of hospitals. You may not remember the experience that implanted why you react to things the way you do, but your subconscious mind has it locked away in your vault and ensures you react that way every time.

This can be pretty scary especially when you think you have control of your emotions and you believe something about yourself consciously, but your body delivers a different message. Have you ever been in a situation where you wanted to come across sure of yourself but then something embarrassing happened? You tried your hardest to remain calm and not show your emotions. You started talking to yourself, telling yourself not to get red in the face. You begged to yourself, "please, please, don't turn red," but then it happened, you felt the hot sensation starting in your neck as it crept up over your entire face, exposing your true feelings.

What happened? You used your conscious mind to give an order, why didn't your subconscious mind react to your request?

The reason was because your subconscious mind has control of you and knows that you embarrass easily so it will send the message loud and clear.

Think of a time at school when the teacher asked a question and you knew the answer. You did not however put up your hand. You toyed with the idea of raising your hand and giving the answer but out of fear you did not do it. Someone else then raised their hand, said the answer you were going to say, and they were right. Why didn't you raise your hand? Even though you wanted to, your subconscious mind told you not to because of your past programming. You may not remember why this doubt was implanted in your mind, but it is there and you are reacting to it without knowing, even when you know you should not.

It is not enough to tell your subconscious mind to react a certain way, it will react the way it is programmed, the way the original emotion was imprinted. Perhaps what happened was a reminder of something in your past and you resonated with the emotion you felt at the time. It would have triggered the emotion of fear; hence you didn't raise your hand. Telling it not to react wasn't enough. Your subconscious mind took over based on your past imprints even though you were not aware of them. Maybe you had an experience where you put yourself out there before and someone made fun of you or made you feel bad and now you have tied that emotion to the action. If you put yourself out there, you will be ridiculed. Whatever the emotion it will be triggered. If you do not replace the new reaction with a new imprint, it will just go back to what is there and spit out the rerun.

Even if you think you believe something to be true, your subconscious mind may already be programmed to send a different message. If you are thinking that saying something to your subconscious mind just once is going to make it believe it you are wrong. This is why so many people have problems with affirmations. They may be saying them here and there, but because they are not repeating it continuously, the subconscious mind does not receive the message. If you do not send the messages continuously, and with emotion, it will continue with the reruns, reacting to things the way it always did before. You have to feel it and believe it.

Until you consciously deliver a new message to your subconscious mind that you never get embarrassed, that you can laugh at yourself, it will show the reruns. You must imbed the new thought over and over again, until the subconscious mind believes it and then delivers your confidence through your actions.

Try and think about things that you currently do without thinking. Are there any things you are doing that do not serve you well? Why do you think you are doing them?

So how do we go on with a new action when we are programmed with so many that we are not even aware of? When you are clear about your vision, you can start looking at what is currently in your life and develop a sense of what is important to you.

If we want to change from who we are now to someone else we need to understand how this paradigm works throughout our bodies. Everything that passes through our mind imprints itself on our cells. Much like light that passes through a lens, it affects the chemical on the film and creates the image. Your image that is created from your mind has to be released and the way your mind does this is through your body.

Your mind emits energy that flows through every part of your body and secretes itself through every cell. In fact, your body is the instrument of whatever image you have formed in your mind, or in other words, the result of the movie you are watching in your mind. Whatever thoughts you have internally are coming out in your body whether you like it or not. Your subconscious mind is running you and deciding for you what movie it will be playing. Your current situation is your body reacting to whatever is in your subconscious mind.

Your thoughts are imprinting images in your mind all the time. If you do not take control of the images being implanted, you go into autopilot and the movies in your vault will project what is already there, in other words, reruns. You will continue to do what you are doing over and over again whether you like it or not.

Here's an example of how an imprint would work. Let's say you are a very good actor and at an audition you are told by the director that you are a terrible actor and that you have no talent. Your conscious mind can either accept or reject the comment. If it accepts it, it sends the message to the subconscious mind that you truly are a bad actor. If you go to numerous auditions and the message is always the same, "you have no talent" you will begin to believe the comments. The subconscious mind then produces the result through your body which may be in the form of shame, low self esteem, and then bad acting. You will become a bad actor no matter how hard you try because your subconscious mind accepted the comment.

Now what if you took control of your conscious mind and rejected the comments. You decided that maybe that particular day you did have a poor performance but that you would be better at the next audition. Perhaps the director didn't use the right words, maybe you were not right for that particular part, your acting did not suit that particular role, but that doesn't mean you are a bad actor. Maybe there is room for improvement and what they said helped you discover something you needed to work on to make your auditions better. Or maybe you just had a bad audition. If you reject the negative comment made to you, the subconscious mind does not accept it. It goes on believing that you are a good actor, you just had a hiccup in your day and you move on to your next performance. Your subconscious mind continues to send your body the image of a good actor. The conscious mind makes the decision on what it will allow into the subconscious mind based on the vision you have in your mind. If you want to act in a movie, that vision doesn't change because of the audition. You accept that you will not be acting in that particular movie and move on.

Your subconscious mind is there to deliver what it is you want. You just need to know how to program it. The great thing about the subconscious mind is that it is pretty gullible. It may be persistent with showing you reruns, but it can be fooled pretty easily.

You see the subconscious mind does not know the difference between a lie and the truth. It will believe whatever you tell it, as long as you imprint the message in it clearly. You must truly feel the emotion for it to be implanted on the subconscious mind.

Imagine the possibilities! You can tell it whatever you want and it has to produce it. The trick is to override the current reruns so that it will project your new movie. Your subconscious mind is set in its ways so you are going to start feeding it your new vision on a continuous basis. You need to gain full control to select and view whatever movie you want to see.

Start by organizing your vault into sections of movies you loved in your life and those you hated. Move the good ones to the front, the movies that make you feel good, stir up great emotions and make you smile. The rest can go on that back shelf for now to collect dust.

The only past movies in your vault that can be used right now are the ones that inspire you and motivate you to reach your goals. The great news is that if there are not enough good ones, you are going to learn to make them.

CHAPTER 5

Appointing Your Director

Many actors in the industry write a script, direct and star in the movie themselves. Woody Allen and Clint Eastwood are two that come to mind.   I'm sure there are many different reasons they may do this. Perhaps they do it for the credit, the money or just to have control. But I believe many do it for more personal reasons. When they write their script, they see themselves in the role, and visualize the final movie in such detail that they cannot let anyone else do it. No one else can see the vision the way they do. They want control of the way the movie will look and feel and they want to make sure their message is delivered the way they intended. In their mind, no other person can portray and recreate their vision other than themselves.

And how many times has their movie turned into the absolute blockbuster of the year? In fact, we say that no other person could have played the part. That is because they wrote the script with themselves as the star.

It's not that they are controlling people (although maybe they are), but they wanted what was projected in their minds to be created the way they saw it, not the way someone else would interpret it.

Pitching an idea to a movie producer is very difficult. A picture has to be portrayed for the executives so that they can form it in their minds and understand the true vision of the movie. The producers have to envision what that message would look and feel like. The better the pitch the better the chance the producers will be sold on the idea. The problem is that they first need to see the vision in their minds.

I often wonder how the Wizard of Oz was pitched to the producers. If it wasn't for the book, how would that idea have been put in words? I know I couldn't explain that movie without sounding absolutely ludicrous. "I have this idea of a girl who gets lost in a tornado and meets a bunch of little people, there are two witches, a wizard, there are talking trees, a scarecrow, a lion and a man made of tin." At a time when color was just being introduced this was quite an order.

The good news here is that you will not be pitching your movie to anyone else; in fact, I recommend you keep your new vision to yourself. You see, before you take this idea out to anyone else, you need to pitch it to the strongest critic out there, yourself.

I remember the story I heard about Sylvester Stallone when he released his blockbuster film "Rocky." He told how he wrote the screenplay and based his character totally as if he was playing the part. He could only envision himself in the role and he wanted to play it. That was his main idea in selling the screenplay. He went from producer to producer and was continually encouraged to sell the script but not with him in the lead. He never budged from his convictions and finally he got the movie made the way he intended, with him as the lead. I don't think anyone would argue, no one else could have played it as well as he did.

The producers could not envision Stallone in the role, but wanted other people to play Rocky. They were tailoring someone else's idea to suit their way of thinking. If Stallone had sold out and let the producers cast someone else, his vision never would have come to fruition.

All of our lives we have tried to project our ideas, thoughts, looks and personalities and we've waited for others to tell us what they think. Well, it really doesn't matter what they think, because they cannot see your vision. Only you can see it. So to try to convince someone of your vision is not going to be productive. The only person you need to convince right now is yourself, or more accurately, your subconscious mind.

At this point you should discover how powerful your mind is. It has had full control of you up until now and it likes things just the way they are. Remember, every result you have produced was because your subconscious mind projected it through you. Whatever it accepts is being projected through your body, so your first order of business is to have it accept your new vision. But much like the producers with Rocky, your subconscious mind has its own visions and that is to project your reruns.

In fact, it is going to do everything in its power to keep you from having a new vision by putting in some reruns to remind you why you can't have a new vision. Every movie has an antagonist, the person who opposes the vision of the main character, and your mind is no different. Your subconscious mind is going to fight you. And this subconscious mind is pretty strong. It has been producing your movies for so long, it is just churning out the same movies over and over and resisting whenever you want to create something new.

How can we take control of something so powerful that has been running who you are for all of this time? It has been telling you how to act and feel for so long that you have no idea how to take control so that you can create what you really want.

It is time to appoint a new director of your new movie, your new vision. This director will face your subconscious mind head on and take control of your projector to continually run your vision. It will ensure that your dream comes true by consistently working your subconscious mind until it not only believes in your vision, it will be on autopilot.

The name of the director of your vision is Will. Okay so I gave your *will* a name, but I hope it helps you with the vision.

You will need to mentally exercise your will. Your will needs to be in charge of this entire production, creating the entire movie, what it looks like and how to project it. You have your script in mind, you just need someone to manage it and make it all happen.

Your will needs to be one tough director. It is so clear on the end result that it knows exactly who and what it needs to be part of this venture.

But just like with any situation, when someone or something else takes over from another, there will be some resistance. Your subconscious mind is not going to like someone else being in charge. It is happy just the way it is, running reruns and slacking off. Your will is going to be putting your subconscious mind to work, forcing it to put a new movie in the projector, your vision, and that is going to take some effort.

Your subconscious mind will fight by running reruns in your mind of why you can't achieve your new goal, how hard it is, and why you aren't worthy of a new goal. It will fill the projector with negative comments about you and how you cannot achieve things and how they are impossible. It will run movies of how you failed in the past, how you aren't able to achieve your goal, and it will tell you that you should just be happy with the way things are.

Remember, your vault has plenty of back-up film to talk you out of this new movie, some bad emotions that your subconscious is going to make you feel and relive. It will tell you that everything is fine just as it is and to stop dreaming! Just like not raising your hand in school when you knew the answer, your past memories are going to take control.

It will also remind you that you are not being good when you are dreaming. That is how you were programmed. Just like when you were in school staring out the window imagining something but you were scolded for day-dreaming. You weren't day-dreaming; you were building your imagination.

You have been conditioned over the years not to imagine. And now I am asking you to imagine and day-dream. Dreams really do come true so you have to start believing that it can happen to you, not just to other people. You need to start dreaming again.

You will know when your subconscious mind is winning and your will is losing because you are going to want to quit. That is your cue to step up. They don't call it "exercising your will" for nothing. You will have to work harder whenever you get the feeling to give up and let your dream die. Just like a new workout regime with weights, you are creating a new program in your mind, and it can be tiring. Fighting your negative emotions is going to be tough. Just remember to use your will when you see the signs of your getting tired of the fight. The same as when you lift weights, there is going to be resistance, but knowing that the more you conquer it, the stronger you will become.

What your subconscious mind is showing you are just past occurrences in your memories, the past movies in your vault. You want a new movie, a new life, a new goal and the way to do that is to understand what you need to do.

Your will has seen your script and is sold on the idea. Your director is ready to put this in action and sees your vision. It is the ally in your movie and not only is your will going to go up against your subconscious mind, it is also going to decide who and what comes through the gate of your studio lot.

Remember your will is focused on your vision and it is ordering your conscious mind, the gatekeeper, to only allow through your five senses the items that will get you closer to your vision.

The director of your production is there to put the vision together by taking away chaos from your lot and creating order. It will be leading you forward to turning your script into a movie. Trust in the power of your will and think about how great it will feel when you get to see the finished product.

I hope you are realizing the importance of having a clear vision, knowing how things work in your mind, and understanding the framework of what resources you have to work before taking on something new.

Now that you have your idea for your script, you have your studio in order with your director and your gatekeeper you can now focus on the production.

CAMERA!

Projecting You

The Protagonist Emerges

CHAPTER 6

Be Careful What You Ask For

I bet if I asked you what the last movie you saw was about, you would be able to tell me quite confidently. You may share with me who the stars in the movie are, how you felt during the different moments and then you would probably go into critiquing mode and advise me on whether it was a good or bad movie and if I should see it.

But if I asked you who produced it, who wrote or directed it, or even better, who the cameraperson was, would you be able to be as forthcoming with an answer? What if I asked you who the set designer or gaffer was, would you know?

Of course you wouldn't. Unless you were involved somehow with that movie or knew someone whose name would be on it you would not care who put the movie together no matter how good it was.

But there they are after every movie, the list of names on the credits, scrolling through the screen one after the other, usually to some form of orchestral music designed to have us exit the theatre at a calm pace. Some producers have added extra scenes or put some entertaining notes during the credits to try and keep us interested, but in the end, we usually dismiss those details because we were there for the end result of all their hard work. We don't want to think about how things were made, we just want to be swept away into a fantasy world for a couple of hours.

What we need to take note of is that in order to put the production we just witnessed on the screen, specialists in hundreds of fields came together to form a perfectly aligned process that in the end created a result, the movie.

They had a clear goal and meticulously put together a message, piece by piece, by forming every word, every sound, and every prop, into one uniform story. It is a perfectly synchronized process that is started months or years before a movie is ever released for the public to view.

There is no doubt that to achieve what you want, the more clearly you focus on the details, the better chance of you getting exactly what you asked for. I believe the universe has a bit of a sense of humor. If you do not take care and be exactly focused on what it is you want, it will fill in the blanks for you and send what it believes you asked for, whether it was what you wanted or not.

There have been many movies made with the "be careful what you ask for" story line. My favourite has to be a movie in the '90s by Penny Marshall called "Big." It tells the story of Josh, who is 13 and struggling to get the attention of a girl he adores, Cynthia. She is much taller than he is and is going with a boy that not only is taller than Josh, but he drives a car. The crushing scene is when at a carnival, Josh, in front of Cynthia is not allowed on a ride because he is too small. Absolutely mortified, he wanders around the carnival in dismay, totally consumed by his emotions. Across the boardwalk he sees an unusual arcade machine. It is the half body of a genie named Zoltar, who with the deposit of a quarter, will grant you any wish you ask. Poor Josh is so upset that he quickly puts in his money, and without thinking clearly, blurts out the words "I wish I was big." Well you can already see the beginnings of a lot of chaos because if I were to ask you what big meant, we could come up with various answers. But in this case it was to be Zoltar's version, not Josh's.

Well his wish was granted. The next day he was big, he was also 30! He became a 13-year-old boy in a 30-year-old's body. Josh got what he asked for, but it was not what he intended.

The universe we currently live in is much like Zoltar. If we ask for something and pay the price it will deliver exactly what you request. But if you are unclear, it will make its own interpretation and send you its version. Remember, we all have been taught the same things but with different perceptions. Just because you say something in general, doesn't mean that the request will be received the way you wanted. The more detail you give, the better chance of your vision being delivered.

When we are unclear about what we really want, we do not get the results we want. We then blame circumstances, other people, or just plain bad luck for the way things go in our lives.

Your goal or vision, whatever it might be, needs to be so precise, in such detail, that when you project it to the subconscious mind, it will know exactly what you intended and deliver the order to you.

For many of us, we know what the movie looks like, but we want it here and now. We become impatient. We get enthusiastic at the start, do the process, but when we don't see the results right away we decide it is too hard and then we quit!

Our movie is taking too long to make so we go back and watch a rerun and justify it with "why create something new when you can just go watch what's already there?"

We don't know how much time and energy will go into the making and delivery of your movie. It is an original and has never been done before. You need to trust that you will complete it and the way to stay focused on it is to keep watching it in your conscious mind, and the way to stay focused on it is to make your movie so exciting and so amazing, you will want to watch it all the time and never go back to your vault. You will not settle for reruns.

The key is to identify exactly what it is you want and to make it your focus.

Just like an Academy Award-winning movie, when all of the details are in alignment and the process goes as planned, the results are amazing.

Because we are creating the vision of your life, and you want it to be perfect, we are going to start producing it just like a movie with every detail taken care of. You may think that you have a dream in your mind that you can see quite clearly, but we need to look at every aspect to make sure you get exactly what you ask for. The universe, much like Zoltar, will send exactly what you ask, so it's best to make it as accurate as possible. You deserve the best so let's start seeing it come to life.

CHAPTER 7

Your Heroic Journey

Before a studio creates a script, they decide on the format for telling their story. One of the most popular is the Hero's Journey. This is where an unsuspecting character minding their own business is placed into a situation out of their control that takes them on a journey of self-discovery. In most cases they end up becoming the hero they never imagined being and are transformed into the new and improved person.

The main character in any journey is called the protagonist. The most famous hero's journey character I can think of is Luke Skywalker in Star Wars. The movie begins with Luke, living and working on a moisture farm on the planet Tatooine, similar to the way a boy would be working on a farm here on earth. He is being raised by his aunt and uncle in a remote area where during most of his day he is doing chores. He is going about his normal life when he comes across a hidden message in a robot and sets out to deliver this important message to the intended party. Through a series of events he not only ends up in a world he has never experienced before, he becomes the hero of the movie by saving an empire from the evil antagonist, Darth Vader. Luke's journey took him from a regular farm boy in a remote location to a Jedi Master of the "Force" in a new empire.

You are similar to Luke Skywalker. As this is all about your journey, you are now the protagonist. See yourself in your ordinary life getting the same results over and over, but you are about to embark into a world where you have never been before, experience things you have never seen before, and in the end be the hero of this adventure.

The difference is that you know it is coming. In preparing your movie you should be thinking about changing something specific and growing one particular part of you into something new.

To see examples of this we need to go to the movies. The next time you watch a movie, pay attention to the growth of the characters. They often hated someone and eventually fell in love with them, didn't know something but then discovered something new, or wanted something and eventually achieved it. There is always a change that happens, good or bad, but it always unfolds. That is how a script is developed.

You as the protagonist must change. This is a natural law of life. We always need to be growing or else we will just be dying. If you are not constantly changing and growing in your life, you will be disintegrating. This is why so many people are unhappy. They have stopped growing as people and are disintegrating.

The only way to keep growing is to use your imagination. We have all used our imagination in the past and have been excited about an idea. Do you remember how wonderful that feeling was when you had a great idea? When you use your imagination and think about something that excites you, it creates a reaction in your body, a vibration, and it is that vibration that is causing the growth in you. Sometimes it is a scared and excited feeling mixed together but that is what you need to be doing. When was the last time you got really excited about an idea?

When you are writing this script for yourself, I want you to be both excited about the idea of obtaining it, and at the same time a bit scared because you don't know how you are going to do it. That is when you know you are moving in the right direction.

You get to decide what movie you want to make and how you will change as the leading character and best of all, how the movie will end.

At this point you need to start looking at how you want to change from who you are now into the individual you see in your mind.

The interesting thing is who you currently perceive yourself to be may be different from the person you want to become. In other words, what personality or trait are you suppressing that you really want to release? There is a script in you and it is just dying to get out. Do you know who you really are deep inside yourself?

We were all born with our own leading part in a script that was written just for us, but we chose to play a supporting role in someone else's movie. We go through life being the people we think others want us to be and lose our true selves in the process.

When I did this exercise I discovered an interesting pattern in my life. For years I wanted to study to be a writer but told myself I wasn't good enough. I looked back into my childhood and realized that I was writing throughout my school years. In elementary school I would write stories for fun, and I wrote a school play. During my teens I continued to write but with one difference. All the poems, stories and jokes I wrote were hidden, tucked away in boxes in a closet. Eventually I destroyed them all. What changed in my life that caused me to go from sharing all of my work to hiding it? Obviously at some point in my life I had decided that I wasn't good at writing and stopped sharing it.

But just like a sleeping volcano, whether I liked it or not, the hidden writer would spew.

When I took a closer look I could see the recurring theme in my life. Every job or situation I was ever in, I incorporated something to do with writing into my daily life. I would create things for volunteer positions, articles, flyers, anything that required writing and creating. At work I would be writing newsletters, lyrics for songs, stories and articles. But the lowest point came when I was writing for other people and watched as they got the credit. That didn't feel good at all. I was willing to be a bit part in someone else's movie rather than play the lead myself.

I made the choice to start playing the lead in my movie and I want you to start doing the same. Writing this book was scary and exciting for me because I had to do what I stopped doing in elementary school. I had to put myself out there and share with others. But I know that in doing this I am growing as a person and releasing that which is inside me. Like a volcano, it has spilled out as a book.

Take a closer look at yourself. What recurring theme do you see of yourself that is coming out all the time that perhaps you have been suppressing?

Where you are now is ultimately because of your past decisions. Remember you are working out your protagonist for the person you want to be. There are no limits here. Your imagination is writing the story for you. You are becoming a hero in this movie, so what does that look like to you? You cannot ask anyone else what that is because they have their own version of what a hero is in their own mind.

Start thinking about who you really are and what you want to accomplish in this life. You should be smiling right now because you finally have permission to think for yourself. If not, go back and really think about a time in your past when something really excited you.

Were you ignited by someone who showed you the potential that you knew was there but never wanted to acknowledge? Did someone spot something in you that you never knew you had, or better yet, you always wanted to develop but were too afraid? Are you waiting to be discovered? This is how many of us live our lives. We are waiting for someone else to come and show us the way. Well, you are the only one in charge of this production. Create whatever it is that you want.

My first signal of who I am is shown through the characters I relate to in a movie. When I connect to someone in a role or to their experience I find that it is because they are touching on an emotion or a situation that I want to have. Many of us can watch the same movie and because of our past experiences in life, relate to different characters in the movies based on our emotions.

For example, let's look at Raiders of the Lost Ark. The protagonist Indiana Jones is the mild- mannered, good-looking teacher by day, but has the ability to turn into the tough, gun-toting thrill-seeker who has hundreds of enemies out to kill him. This is a determined man who in either role knows what he wants and goes after it without anything getting in his way, including women. His perseverance and focus is so undeterred that danger is just part of the job. He lives and breathes antiquities and will risk his life to protect and preserve them. Nothing will stand in his way.

And then there is Marion, the daughter of Indiana's mentor. Marion always finds herself playing a role in someone else's dream. Indiana, being true to his nature and going after what he wanted with determination, took advantage of Marion at a young age causing a rift between Marion, her father and Indiana. Marion then was forced to travel with her father on his quests until his passing, which left her stranded in a foreign country, becoming a rough, hard-drinking bar owner, trying to find her way back to her normal life in the United States. She once again becomes a supporting role, this time to Indiana, being dragged around the country while he pursues his quests, only to find she is abandoned again and having to fend for herself.

Which character do you find yourself resonating with? Which character did you see as yourself now or the person you want to be? When you really look closely at a character that you empathize with you can find qualities about yourself that maybe you did not know existed.

Are you determined and go after what you want in life? Will you do it at any cost even at the expense of others? Are you passionate about something or an activity that you want to make the focus in your life?

Do you want to be admired and respected and treated like an expert in your field much like Indiana Jones? Will you study and devote all of your time and energy to acquiring that expertise?

Or maybe you see yourself as a treasure that someone in the world will do anything to find. Will you allow someone to find you or have you surrounded yourself with traps and made it too risky of an attempt?

Perhaps you are going through life doing what you have to do to survive and are waiting for someone to come save you. Are you willing to keep waiting and playing a part in someone else's dream with the hopes that you may find what you are looking for?

You are going to be scripting your character in such a way that your final destination is going to be clear to you. You will have no choice but to become the character and begin creating your new role in life.

Take a look at the movies you currently love, the ones you have watched over and over again. What is it about that movie that you felt, that sparked an emotion that made you feel good? Really take a look at the character that you relate to and you may discover something about yourself you never really knew was there. It may be the one thing you need to bring into your movie so that you can finally reveal the real you.

If I had to describe Indiana Jones it would be persistent. He never waivers from this characteristic throughout the movie, he just never gives up. You too have a characteristic that is the core of who you are. Do you know what that might be?

When you watch the characters more closely it may reveal a pattern and make you aware of the person you are inside. Whatever it is about that person you are admiring and respecting, is the quality you hold within yourself, that's why you see it and resonate with it, good or bad.

The more you know about your character in this movie, the better you can write your script. Much like Indiana Jones, you are the hero. Right now, the only person that needs to see that is you.

CHAPTER 8

What Genre Are You?

As social creatures, people tend to congregate with others who have similar interests or characteristics. We are attracted to particular people, places and events in our lives because they give us a certain feeling. We tend to bond with those that share our thoughts, interests or goals and we interact with them because they make us feel happy.

Movies, much like people, have a way of being categorized, so that they can project to a certain group of people. A movie is made with a certain mood in mind to attract people who want to have that emotion transmitted to them for a couple of hours. Examples of movie genres would be comedy, western, horror, romance, sci-fi or fantasy. Scripts are written and performed based on the emotion the director wants to get from the audience. If they want to scare you, they will create a thriller. If they want to lighten up your mood they will create a comedy. Many producers mix genres to make things more interesting in the story lines and this in turn will attract a more varied audience.

I find that people can be labeled with a genre much like a movie. If you take a look around you, can you label someone as a comedy, or a drama? How about a romance or a thriller? When you pay attention you can see how we are not only one specific genre, we tend to mix a couple of them together.

Have you ever wondered what "genre" you are? What emotional genre can you see in yourself?

If you really thought about yourself and your true personality, what "genre" would you like to be? We, much like a movie, need to know our "mood." How do you like to feel and what sparks your energy?

I believe that when we are living in our true genre, we will be more productive and acquire more happiness in life. If you can be clear about what type of personality you are, you will be clearer in what you want to surround yourself with.

It is very important for us to discover what our natural genre is inside before we place ourselves in relationships or careers. What genre will allow you to grow to your full potential?

What if you are a very serious person that likes to get things done and wants to be around others who are focused on their work? Can you imagine being put in a room with a bunch of comedians throwing one-liners around the room and distracting everyone? How would this make you feel? You would not be in your natural light achieving what you wanted, and you would not be enjoying it at all.

I want you to be reasonable with this idea. If you are currently in a position that is a drama, but you are a comedy, you can implement some comedy in your life, you just need to be aware of the boundaries in your situation. It doesn't have to be black or white. You can learn to incorporate who you are with other situations and make them a comedy/drama. The situation continues but you incorporate a little bit of fun to appease those who need it but not enough that it affects the others. Just like a movie merging two genres, it works and it appeals to a broader audience.

But what if the genre of your job or your relationship contradicts who you truly are and you begin conforming to the genre or the mood of the other person? What if you are asked, or even worse, forced to become a genre that is not you?

If you find yourself in a relationship for example with someone and you cannot be your true self, the effects of this will start coming through you in a negative way. If we can't release our natural feelings and we suppress them, they back up and eventually explode and it will be released through the body as a negative response, action or illness.

We all need to express who we truly are by being in the right performance. You don't ask a clown to perform in a courtroom. If you want to be a clown all the time, go find a place where clowns get rewarded for being clowns all the time. You don't ask the courtroom to turn into a circus.

It is when we start demanding others to conform to our genre that we cross the line. We are now asking others to relinquish themselves to achieve our dreams and our goals.

The purpose of our lives is to grow but to do it in a way that does not impose on others. We need to understand the boundaries. If you cannot mix the genres, move on to another person or job.

When you use this analogy of genres and compare it to individual personalities, morals or ethics, you can start seeing where some problems are arising in your life. You cannot write the script of your life without first identifying the genre you want to have.

For example, if you are a people person, an animated individual that loves to socialize, working in a cubicle eight hours per day may just drive you mad. You will find ways to talk to people to make your day more enjoyable, which may distract others around you. You may want to find a business that allows you to talk to people freely. Or what about the drama that is in your office? There is that one person who has to go into every small detail of their life into an hour-long story of woe. Do you chime in or do you try and get away?

Sometimes you just need to adjust your current situation. Behave accordingly but make sure you know your boundaries. What is your boundary? At what point is your "self" being controlled by someone else, where your true productivity or "self" goes down.

Many people compromise what they believe in for the sake of a pay cheque or a reward. They settle doing something that is against what they stand for thinking that they have no choice.

When we bottle up our true feelings, they come out eventually in a negative form. Don't under-estimate your body. It will release it whether you like it or not. It will be in the form of skin conditions, excess weight, or illness. You name it, the deeper your frustration, the stronger the release.

We are all capable of thinking we are doing something for a good reason, and we can rationalize it, but whatever is in the core of your being will eventually find a way to take over.

I can think of a classic movie that describes two people madly in love, but because of their difference in personalities and beliefs, cannot be together. The movie is "The Way We Were" with Barbara Streisand and Robert Redford.

Katie and Hubble are about as far apart on the personality scale as you can imagine. Hubble is always smiling, enjoying life, seeing the humor in everything. He loves to laugh and is one of those people where things are just always handed to him, things just come easily. Katie on the other hand is more serious, always wanting to change and improve things, fighting for the causes and the people she believes in.

The movie follows them on their journey as they attempt to stay together and conform to each other's personalities.

Katie is always pushing Hubble to believe in himself and to try harder for what he wants in life, which is to be a writer. He eventually writes his book and ends up in Hollywood very successful. Unfortunately, Hubble is not happy as he finds he needs to learn to fight, not only for his job but also for his wife. He is forced outside of his natural character which in the end makes him miserable. He stops laughing and enjoying life.

Katie on the other hand learns to be the subdued socialite and conforms to Hubble's idea of what a woman should be. She tries to keep her mouth shut but eventually cannot control it any longer and gets back into the fight for her country and the rights of people.

Hubble, desperately wanting a woman who is happy with being a socialite and riding the carefree life, has an affair with his ex girlfriend. Katie, feeling suffocated, goes back to being the fighter of the causes she believes in knowing it is not what Hubble wants. The need to be their true selves was stronger than their love for each other. No matter how hard they tried, they could not contain it. They both went through the relationship suppressing their true characters in order to please the other but in the end their true nature had to be released. Sometimes mixing two genres just doesn't work.

Who do you know right now who is living in a drama, or even worse a suspense/thriller? Do you know someone who was always happy and bright but is now in a job or a marriage where they are being abused verbally or worse, physically? Have you seen the laughter and the happiness leave this person and see it now replaced with fear and regret? This is an example of a person making another one conform to their genre. The abuser is a suspense/thriller needing to control and send the message of fear throughout their life. They have crossed the boundary and made another individual live in their genre. A boss that constantly yells or puts down an individual at work in front of co-workers is another example. This person is making everyone live in his genre. How do you think that helps the productivity of his workers? Unless the staff thrives in that type of atmosphere, anyone who does not feel right in that job will leave. Turnaround would be incredible.

The movie Horrible Bosses took a comedic approach to this theory. Three different individuals working under unbearable circumstances are tested daily by their irrational bosses to behave in ways that did not resonate with their true selves. Their lives were full of despair, anxiety and unhappiness. The end result was, they formed so much negativity towards their bosses that their only way out was to murder them. This of course being a comedy took a humorous spin but the analogy is true to life. When we are put in a continuous situation that does not resonate with our true selves, we stop thinking productively and start acting unproductively.

When you are clear about who you are and what you stand for, you have a better chance of finding what you want. Know clearly before you set your intention for this vision exactly who you are and what situation do you want to find yourself.

You can find a hint of the genre you are by the movies you like to watch. What emotion do you like to have triggered at the theatres? Are you the thrill seeker who needs to be sparked by watching action adventure movies?

Perhaps you are the happy-go-lucky individual who wants to feel the warmth and comfort of a romantic comedy. Melodramas, animations, fantasy. They are all geared to a certain audience.

Make a list of your favourite movies. That may be the first sign of your genre just trying to peek out.

This concept can be applied to your work and to your personal relationships. When you are clear about what genre you are, what mood you want to be projecting, you will more easily be able to envision your movie.

You are now creating a new movie with no previous constraints. You are the star. You are choosing the genre right now and your movie will be projecting that emotion to the universe. Be clear on how you want to feel in your vision.

If you are not the star in your current movie, this may be a good time to check your admission ticket. You may be sitting in the wrong theatre.

CHAPTER 9

Special Effects

We were each born with our own unique look and personality. We accepted who we were because we didn't know anything different. Over time however we have learned to compare ourselves to other people and decided in our minds what is normal and what is not. This is almost impossible to do, because who decided what is normal? We are all different colours, shapes and sizes. You may share something similar with another person, or have the same characteristic or trait, but there is no exact replica of you. I believe we are confusing "normal" with "social acceptance."

There are many actors and comedians who became famous because of their individuality or their quirkiness. These people did something that most of us won't. They learned to accept their difference and use it as their strength and not as a weakness. Rather than seeing their difference as a detriment and changing it, they capitalized on it and made it brighter. The way they acted or looked was not what at the time was socially accepted, but once it was introduced to us, and we became accustomed to it, it was accepted.

But before these individuals introduced themselves to the world, they had to first learn to accept themselves.

No other person in the world looks, sounds, acts and thinks just like you. Even twins can have something different. I like to call this individuality your "special effect."

When someone sees and hears you for the first time you are having an effect on them. You are sending to them, without even knowing, the energy of who you are. This is the first time the person has ever met one of you. It is their first time to experience anything like it in the world. It is like discovering a new species. You truly are one of a kind.

But how many times do you find yourself holding back, not being who you want to be, or shying away because of the fear of what someone might think of you or that you will be judged? This is a common trait amongst us because of our trying to fit into the "normal" category. What we need to understand is that until we accept ourselves, no one else will.

The only thing keeping you from expressing your "special effect" is your confidence.

If I were to ask you to name a comedian in a movie who created an "original one of a kind character," who would that be?

My first choice has to be Jim Carrey. I remember when I first saw him in Ace Ventura: Pet Detective. He had so many rubber-faced expressions, voices and one-liners I like the rest of the world was totally amazed at how funny he was. I had never seen anything like it before. Can you imagine if he had decided that his expressions were silly and that he was too embarrassed to do them in public because he hadn't seen anyone else do them? How many wonderful characters and movies would we have been cheated out of seeing? But he did what he planned to do and we all were blessed with his entertainment. He understood that his "special effect" was extraordinary and he used it to his advantage.

But it is easy for us to sit back and judge his success. We start by outlining what he has that we do not. What special thing or quality he had that made him famous and because we don't have it, we will never be as successful as him.

Isn't that interesting how we do that? We say that people had luck, a special talent or look but we never see that for ourselves. The only difference between them and you is that they had the confidence to pursue their dream despite what any one else said. They learned to accept themselves as who they wanted to be and they didn't let anything stand in their way. They focused on what they wanted in life and not on what they didn't want.

If you want to start expressing confidence in yourself you have to first accept yourself for you who are and your unique person.

There is a difference between not liking something and not accepting it. You don't have to like a certain body part, the sound of your voice or the way your hair is, but you can learn how to accept it. If you accept yourself, others will start accepting you.

Many of us see something in ourselves that is the cause of all our frustration. It is a flaw that we have or a situation in our life that is holding us back from achieving the goal we want in life. We have decided that what we want is unattainable because of this one thing and if only it were not there, life would be good. Does this sound familiar?

The truth is that what we want is attainable, but we have justified in our minds that we will never achieve it because of this obstacle.

We need to eliminate what we believe is the problem from our minds and replace it with the positive. If you have a feature that to you is distracting and affecting your appearance, you have probably put so much focus on it that you have made it more prominent. It is all you see and therefore your body is going to project it in the form of making sure it is all other people see as well. When your focus is on your negative, you are actually covering up other positive things about yourself. You are eliminating the good things and replacing them with your so called "bad thing" and making that the first thing people see in you. You will be projecting the negativity as your special effect.

I think the best story to illustrate this point has to be Cyrano De Bergerac. Cyrano was a charming character, a swordsman, respected by everyone, but he suffered from one enormous problem, a nose so large that every person that came in contact with him froze in shock at the sight of it.

This film has been made a couple of times but the most recent depiction was by Steve Martin in the movie "Roxanne."

The main character C. D. Bales is the local town fire chief, willing to face any challenger to a duel of wit should they ever mention the size of his nose. C. D. is so consumed by his flaw it keeps him from pursuing his true love, the new girl in town, Roxanne.

Things get worse for C. D. when he finds out that not only is Roxanne in love with a man that works for him, she wants C. D. to introduce them.

The love interest, a complete bumbling idiot that cannot put a phrase together, asks C. D. to write love letters to Roxanne on his behalf. C. D. jumps right in for the chance to write Roxanne his true feelings for her without her ever having to know it was him.

Sadly, Roxanne falls deeply in love with the idiot not because of his looks or personality, but because of the letters. C. D. is forced to watch from the sidelines as the other man wins the approval of his one true love.

This movie illustrates so clearly the importance of being yourself. What we see as a flaw may sometimes be an obstacle that we have created in our own minds. When we allow our strengths to take over despite our flaws we allow our true selves to come through and take center stage.

If C. D. had only shared his true self with Roxanne from the start, all this pain and suffering would never have happened. In the end Roxanne discovers who the true author of the letters is, and falls in love with C. D. despite his nose. She was in love with the author of the letters, the soul of C.D., and therefore didn't see the size of his nose as an obstacle. It was just part of who he was.

You need to clearly take a look at your special effects. What talent or ability do you have that you have been hiding because you see it as unusual?

This ability or trait is special only to you. You need to harness this energy and let it emit through you to shine brightly. Just like Edison, when you capture the power, control it and release it, you will fill the room with more light.

What you may have considered a flaw may actually be what someone else thinks is extraordinary. You were given that effect so that people will notice you. Take that as a sign that you have a message to deliver. This doesn't just have to be a physical feature it can be your ability to do something physically or intellectually.

For example, if you love to clean and organize but people have always made fun of you because of this quality, you will suppress it because of the negative spin they have put on it. You start apologizing for being anal or controlling. But there are thousands of disorganized people in the world who cannot clean their own desks. Your talent and ability that you have masked as being a flaw is actually a gift in someone else's eyes. Start being proud of your difference and begin to find a way to express it. Your natural ability may seem like a detriment to some, but can actually be a treasure to someone else.

Pay attention to what is on your list of qualities. When you do this you may understand why you are frustrated with where you are today. When you are not living your true self and not expressing what comes to you naturally, you are blocking your true nature that is trying desperately to come out and help you grow as an individual.

Think about your qualities when you think about your movie and your goal. Really focus on the traits that are important to you. You will learn why you may be unhappy right now in your current role.

This is an important exercise and it can really help you know who you are now and where you want to go. If being your true self is not acceptable in your current situation, then you need to find a situation where it can be expressed freely. You will be happier, more accepting of yourself and in turn, your positive energy will flow from you more brightly.

Embrace your special effect, that look or trait that no one else has, and accept it into your script. Remakes of other movies come and go, but it is usually the original that becomes a classic.

CHAPTER 10

Dressing the Part

How important are first impressions to you? Have you ever judged someone because of the clothes they wear, or been judged that way yourself?

One of the most crucial roles in making a movie is the decision of wardrobe. Clothing and how it's worn tells more about a person than you may think.

Have you ever walked into a high-end store ready to spend lots of money, but were ignored because of your appearance? Maybe it was your day off and you were wearing old shorts and a t shirt and your favorite flip flops. Have you ever been shopping and someone thought you were an employee and asked you for help? Maybe you looked official or you were wearing a shirt the same color that the staff in that particular store wears.

Then there is the perception we have of others. Have you ever paid hundreds of dollars per hour for a professional's services and when you met them they were in a t-shirt and jeans? Were you put off because you expected someone to be dressed professionally and their casual dress gave you the impression they did not take their job seriously?

You can also look at love interests. Did you ever turn down a date with someone because of the way they dressed? I remember a lady telling me that she turned down a date with a man because she did not like the shoes he wore!

Your image and the wardrobe you choose play a major part in your new role. Your wardrobe needs to project an accurate picture of what your vision is all about but not only show you what you what you want to look like, it should also tell some details about who you are, your style and your personality. If a picture tells a story, what story is the picture of you telling?

By looking at your vision, there should be enough clues that if you broke them apart piece by piece you could identify who you are as a person, what you do and what you have.

Remember, the more detail you can provide, the clearer the picture will be in your mind.

At first glance we should be able to know generally who you are. If you are in a suit, we can assume that you are a professional, perhaps a business person, lawyer, advisor, salesperson, etc. If you are in a uniform, the type of uniform would fit exactly the part you are playing in your vision. Are you a doctor, nurse or pharmacist? Each category would have its own distinguishing clue. Are you in a business suit, swimsuit, ski suit, or your birthday suit? The clearer you are about the person you want to become, the more detail you need to provide in your movie.

Let's say your vision is to be a business owner and you want to break away from your job and start your own company. In your current role you wear jeans and runners every day and you rarely see clients face to face. You work on a computer all day and never meet anyone in person so it really doesn't affect your status. But what if your new vision is to be a professional, meeting clients face to face and projecting an image of success? What do you see yourself wearing? Are you now in a nice business suit? Think about the image you want to project and what you want to advertise about yourself. See yourself in this new image.

Once you understand your wardrobe, you also want to add your own style and image. For example are you classy or casual, formal or informal, colourful or subdued? Many of us go through life buying clothes that we can afford, so we have a hard time imagining ourselves in anything else. If your new vision is to be wealthy, then you can begin to visualize yourself in whatever designer clothes you choose. Tailored or off the rack, this is your vision. Make it how you want it with no boundaries.

And don't stop with the clothes, you also need to think about the accessories like glasses. Are you wearing sun glasses, designer frames or maybe no glasses at all? Perhaps you've worn glasses all your life and see yourself with clear vision. This is your goal so make it how you want.

They say you can judge a person by the shoes they are wearing. In your vision, are you wearing leather shoes, sandals, or no shoes at all? Depending on what you are doing in your new role, perhaps living by the beach and having sand in your feet is the final outcome you are envisioning.

What about your body and stature? Are you stronger, more muscular, thinner, more toned? Many of us dream of being in great shape, a smaller size, or being able to hire a personal trainer. Maybe your goal is to teach others to stay fit. How do you look in your vision? Your body image is just as important as how you dress.

By this quick snapshot you should be able to tell at a glance the person you are.

Really use your imagination to find the exact look you want. We all tend to have our own unique style and personality and by adding that to our wardrobe you can be more of yourself. Being and projecting who you truly are will give you a sense of confidence so you want to see yourself as you truly are inside.

Even your hair needs to be addressed. The style, the cut, the colour all contribute to your image. Hair sends a message about who you are as much as your clothing does so really take the time to think about your hairstyle. Is it clean cut, trendy, funky, fun or laid back? Are you currently hiding under a style you are afraid to change or wanting a style but are afraid to try it? This is your head and if you want to shave it in your vision, this is your chance. Finally see yourself in your mind the way you have always wanted to be. Your entire image needs to flow from top to bottom.

Because we are using as much detail as we can, once you figure out how you are dressed, you need to add clues about the person you are, your status and what's important to you. For example, if you are in a uniform, is it decorated with medals, badges or awards? If you are in the military these items display your rankings and tell the story of where you have been and what you have achieved.

Your jewelry is another aspect that can show a lot about what is important to you. What necklace if any are you wearing? Is it a locket with a picture of your kids, a string of pearls, or a rosary? Do you have on a wedding ring, a custom diamond ring, or no ring at all? Maybe you have a pin that represents a cause or group, or a sash that shows a title or a designation.

This is where you need to add as much to your image to give away little hints about who you are, what you represent. You are dressing the part of who you want to become so we want to know as much about you in one glance as possible. Really focus on how you want others to see you as if you had only one shot at revealing yourself. We want to ensure there is no confusion or misconception about who you are in the vision.

I think the best movie example I could use to show the importance of wardrobe would have to be a scene in the movie "Chaplin" where Robert Downey Jr. is re-enacting the time when Charlie Chaplin needed to put his image together to portray his character "The Tramp." Remember, he created a character in a movie with no sound. We had to know everything about this person solely through his image. He is in the wardrobe department meticulously going through every hat, shirt, jacket, pants and shoes to find the right look for the part. Chaplin knew he wanted to portray this person as one who hangs on to his past status, a proud man, but at the same time it was obvious that his clothes were put together by scavenging.

The final result is that the proud man has his top hat, cane and tails, but they are ill-fitting, and mismatched. His wardrobe alone tells us the story that he once was established but is now a tramp.

What wardrobe do you see yourself wearing in your vision? What is the image you want to portray? The more detail the better.

If you find yourself struggling with not being comfortable in your new vision remember it is all just a starting point and that you can add your personality to the style as well. If your new role requires you to be in a suit, but you find them stuffy, you can add your personality to it any way you want. See something whimsical and bright. Replace your regular tie with a bow tie.

Just like genre, you can mix your styles to reveal a little about who you are. Your final character needs to be clear in your mind and project the image you hold of yourself. The more detail you can see the more easily you will portray the part.

When we capture who we really are we do not only look the part we begin to feel it and it is that emotion that we want to always have in the mix.

ACTION!

Your Vision in Motion

The Energy Process

CHAPTER 11

Learning to Act

We are at a crucial part of your movie being made. You know your part, you know how you want to look, but now you need to become the part. How do you do that? You have your conscious mind using your imagination to build your image, and it's trying to get the subconscious mind to change the old movie and put the new movie into the projector.

This is difficult if you are not used to working this muscle in your mind. Once the subconscious mind gets the new movie into the projector, it will play the new movie over and over until your body begins to be that movie unconsciously. You will have become the new movie.

When we introduce our senses into the process of achieving our results, we are using our emotions and our bodies to help our subconscious form the new movie. Instead of just using our conscious mind to impress our new vision with our imagination, we can also trigger our body to feel our expected actions. By doing this we are sandwiching the subconscious mind and forcing it from all directions to see the new movie. The more senses we use, the stronger the impression.

We know that visualizing is causing us to get a new feeling which in turn will emit it through our actions. How can we stir up the emotions inside of us so that our body reacts faster?

To do this we need to go to the professionals, people who do this every day and study the art of acting. We need to look at actors.

Have you ever watched a movie and there was this brilliant actor who was so true to the part, you were convinced they weren't acting but just being themselves? It never ceases to amaze me how great actors can pull me into their fantasy and make me believe they are the character they are portraying.

The truth of the matter is that the ones who make it look easy are the ones who either have a natural ability, or have spent years mastering their craft, in most cases it is the latter.

Whenever I hear an actor wanting to grow by playing another genre, I have to admire and respect them for not becoming complacent. They understand that if they do not keep challenging themselves they will deteriorate. They need to be in constant growth.

You may have heard about those actors that study the "method" form of acting. In this discipline, the actor changes his mind to believe they physically are the character they are portraying by immersing themselves in the person so much that they are not really acting so much as becoming the individual. They look and feel the person they are portraying. Some actors become so entranced in their new character that they continue the performance even when they go home at the end of the day. There have been many stories about actors who were portraying dark characters and because they were always in their part, their personal relationships suffered. Depending on the role, this could be a startling turn of events for their families when their loved one leaves and a stranger returns home.

But it's effective, and it gets results. This is an extreme example of visioning. When our imagination is activated it will send the message to our bodies and it has to emit what we send through action. If I am studying to be a villain who kills and robs banks, then I will look, feel and act like a villain in everything I do. If I am a happy-go-lucky individual, then I will look, feel and act this way in everything. Method acting is internalizing the character and portraying it so that the actions are emitted more naturally.

You have this ability. All you have to do is plant the vision by using your imagination. To make your vision come about, you need to become a method actor.

You have your role and your vision, now you need to practice your lines, and study your material until you know the part by heart. We are showing our subconscious mind the movie we want in our projector by repeatedly causing our vision to be played with our imagination until the subconscious reacts and starts causing the body to conform. But to really speed things up, we can send the subconscious mind there right away by being the physical result as well.

To become the role, you first need to see what the role looks like. The mistake most people make when visualizing is that they watch themselves in the new role they want to portray but as a spectator. They see themselves from a distance as the observer rather than feeling the part as a participant. This is not the way to properly visualize. If you do this you will always just be watching, never doing. This is a common mistake people make and it is this detail alone why many people are not getting results in their lives.

You need to adjust your point of view and see things from your eyes, your viewfinder, as if you were in the role.

For example, if you want to be a public speaker, you need to visualize yourself on the stage looking out at the crowd, not as a person in the audience watching you on the stage.

Start by picturing yourself backstage, you pull the curtain back a bit and you see your audience anxiously awaiting your arrival. Imagine you are introduced and you walk out and shake the hand of your presenter. You turn, and you look down at the faces of the people in the crowd. See the acceptance and the praise you are receiving from the audience and how they applaud you for your great performance. If you are imagining correctly it will stir up the feeling inside you as if it really happened. It is that emotion that you are feeling that will cause the reaction in your body.

When you step into the person who is acting the role, it is a totally different point of view from seeing yourself in the role as an onlooker. If you see yourself from the point of view of the audience, you will never be the one on the stage, you will always be watching. You want to feel the actual experience, which means seeing the audience from the stage.

Your subconscious mind is now surrounded. It has your conscious mind projecting the image of what you want through your visioning, and your body feeling the emotions. Eventually your subconscious mind, not knowing what is real or not, will give up and project the image through you naturally. You will become a public speaker and be more relaxed and confident because you believe it to be so.

You will know when the subconscious mind has taken over, because you will be doing it naturally, without thinking, it will just happen. You will have shifted your paradigm into the new image and you will become that person without thinking any more. It won't be a struggle and your confidence will rise. Use this exercise for any physical activity you want to perform.

If you are an athlete visualize yourself doing the motion you want to happen. A goalie would see the image of the players in front as the puck comes toward the goal and he makes the save. If you are a long distance runner you would see the finish line ahead and see the crowd waiting and cheering as you pass through the ribbon. You need to visualize so clearly that you can feel yourself in the action.

It works the same way with objects. For example, if your vision through the viewfinder is to see yourself as a millionaire living in Monte Carlo, driving down the mountain in your sports car, do not look at yourself from afar driving, feel yourself in the car looking out the windshield, holding the leather steering wheel, looking at your dashboard and out the windshield at the spectacular view of the city. You need to become the part and view it like you are really driving. When you get emotionally involved you attract what it is you want a lot faster.

This is the one step that people do incorrectly and spend their lives wondering why they are not attracting the things they want.

This practice is a lot of fun and can stir up emotions you forgot you had inside. It is also a bit of work to do this regularly. For many, they start visualizing, do not get the instant results, get tired of waiting then tell themselves it is all a waste of time.

The interesting thing with this concept is that when your back talk starts, when you start telling yourself it doesn't work, you may talk yourself into quitting and just go back to the old movies in the vault. When this happens, and it will, be aware that this is your subconscious mind's last-ditch effort to talk you into running the old movies. You are at the "convincing" stage of transforming your subconscious mind to accept the new movie, and it is going to give you one last block with all it has to talk you out of it. This last push from your subconscious mind is usually a very strong one, and most times it wins. It's like it has been saving up its energy to come back at you with one large slam. This is when most people quit.

See this as a turning point. When this struggle is very intense, this is the cue for you to step up to the part with even more vigor. If you break through this "giving up" feeling there is a result at the end. It is like a new energy is trying to manifest and it is sucking out all of your present energy, but instead of accepting the feeling and understanding that the effect is coming, we become totally exhausted, and quit. It is that last burst of energy that your body needs to bring light to the situation. This is where the result is waiting.

Work through it, step back and relook at things in a different way. Tell yourself to be patient because the burst will come. Your faith in this process has to be very strong. You need to believe in yourself and in your idea. Your focus is on the thought and you can see the end result. When you feel this wall of doubt, know that your result is on the other side.

For example, you have a dream of becoming a commissioned sales person. You know that you are a hard worker and will give it 100%. In turn you will make many thousands of dollars and buy your dream home, but a few months in, you find yourself struggling. The sales aren't coming as fast as you had hoped, the costs of running your business are outweighing the commissions coming in, and you watch as your bank account goes into the negative. You know this was your dream and you decided you were going to throw yourself into it, but now you have doubt.

This is usually the time where the subconscious mind slowly takes over. It starts with the back talk, telling you this was a stupid idea, you should get a normal job and to stop thinking you had what it took to be a great salesperson. Everything around you is proof that you should quit and your mind is convincing you it is in your best interest to stop dreaming.

This is where you need to see that the subconscious mind is doing a last push to make you quit. There is no problem with the dream or with sales. The problem is that you have forgotten to stay focused on your vision.

This is where your conscious mind needs to take charge of your thinking and tell the subconscious mind that you are in fact a great sales person. See this as your cue to step up the positive reinforcement you need to get to your goal. Use your will to change the rerun, put your new movie into the projector, and show your subconscious mind that you mean business.

Remember why you wanted to be a salesman in the first place and fill yourself with the images that will make things positive again. Then and only then will you break free from the negative thoughts. Know that the results are coming and keep working towards the vision.

Another tactic you may attempt at this point when confronted by this block is to begin to make changes to your original vision and your script. You decide that maybe if you just make a few adjustments, give up on a few of the ideas, stop being so demanding, maybe it will manifest. You start to justify that you were dreaming too big and if you just make the dream smaller, it will happen. This is another big mistake people make. They stop the dream half-way through and never trust that it will be realized.

When you change your mind, you are actually stopping everything dead in its tracks. You think you are making things easier but all you are doing is confusing the process. This is your deep subconscious mind telling you that you do not deserve your initial thought, forcing you to change your vision. This deflates your energy and turns off your motivation. You have now stopped the energy, that exciting strong energetic flow that is needed to attract what you want. You are adjusting it to a lower level, a weaker level, and in turn you will attract a weaker result.

The thing about the movie in your mind is that you have to have it fixed in place. If you start changing it during the process your mind will get confused and you will not make any progress.

Imagine a movie set that is all ready to shoot a scene with two people sitting in chairs across from each other. The director has the actors seated in position, with the cameras positioned for close ups, the lighting just right on their faces, and the microphones nicely out of sight. The director calls "action" and during the scene one of the actors improvises and decides to stand up for the shot. For whatever reason, the actor feels that the character should now pace rather than sit when delivering the dialogue. The actor bangs his head on the microphone, the cameras are not ready to follow him, and the lighting is not on him any longer. In the end neither the director nor the actor gets the result they expected.

The problem here isn't whether the change in the scene is a good idea or not. The problem is that all the time and energy went into the scene to get a certain result based on the original plan and it was stopped dead in its tracks. It created chaos, slowed the entire process and caused the whole cast and crew to have to start from the beginning again.

When a script is designed and written from the start the way the director intended, then no changes will ever need to be made. The actors would have to do it the way the director intended and the process will run much smoother.

Stick to your initial vision, your scripted lines and trust that the more you follow it, the better your results.

CHAPTER 12

The Vision: Shot by Shot

When a director is given a movie, they must first take time to plan out how they want to shoot it. Before filming even takes place, the director meticulously thinks out the entire movie and how they want it to look, feel and unfold.

There are so many components, staff and equipment that have to come together to make the result happen, without some sort of order there would be extreme chaos. The director is responsible for managing all the pieces so that they come together in the end. To save money and time, it's crucial they be as detailed and organized as possible.

Movies are shot firstly by scenes, events in the story line that happen in each location and then each scene is done in a series of smaller shots. These shots can be at different angles, close or far away, and must contain all of the people and props required to deliver the intended message. For a serious scene the actors' faces can be shown close up, and for a more conversational shot they can be from farther away.

If you were watching a movie about a doctor performing an operation in a hospital, there would need to be a clear message in a series of shots to show you that scene. For you as a viewer to clearly understand the message, a series of shots may be done, one showing the outside of the hospital with the name, the operating room door, the doctor in the room with his bloody hands operating, and the patients face. It is through a series of shots that you get the entire message and you understand clearly who is being operated on and where.

The shooting of the film is so precise, the director will map out a shot-by-shot series of pictures in advance outlining exactly what each will be, who and what are in it.

Each shot is drawn out as a picture, showing clearly what the final outcome should look like, what is happening in the shot and where it is located. Anyone involved in the shoot gets a clear picture of the intention of the director. This outline is called a storyboard.

Without a storyboard, there would be no order on the lot, the cast and crew wouldn't know what scene to shoot, in what order, and who was in it. When a script is finished, the storyboard is the accompaniment that shows everyone how the script will unfold. It is the diagram to the action and dialogue. There is no chaos. This is such an important step that directors have spent months, sometimes years, perfecting their storyboard.

Anyone involved in that final outcome must be in the studio to make that vision happen. If their shot has an actor driving a car, everyone involved in the production needs to see what that final vision looks like so that on the day of the shoot they can recreate that image as it shows on the storyboard. They know where everything is to be placed, what angle to point the camera and the desired outcome. They have a clear image of their desired result. There is no deviation. They have a blueprint image of what the end result looks like and they begin to put in motion the process to obtain that result.

Your mind creates your results in the same way. Your conscious mind creates the image of what you want to achieve, the subconscious mind sees that image, and puts into production that image through you by your actions.

You could speed up the process of achieving your final outcome if you could form an outline as well. As you are currently making a movie in your mind, it is only expected that you make your own storyboard.

You should have a final drawing of what your vision looks like. If you can see your image you will know exactly what it looks like and you will take away any chaos from your mind. There will be no guessing, no deviations, and you will spend your time on making the final shot happen.

You can do this by creating a visual of your images for your eyes to see on a regular basis. This is called a vision board. A vision board is a compilation of photos and images that show your vision as a final product. It doesn't matter what you create or how you create it, as long as it projects the final emotions you want to feel and see when you reach it.

This can be created in a number of ways you just need to find what works for you to get you emotionally connected. For example, if you wanted to create a wall vision board, you can take some cardboard or construction paper and attach photos and items that depict your vision. If your vision is to restore an old Italian Villa, surround your board with pictures of landscape views that you will see from your villa, the trees, the type of flooring in the home, the kitchen and how you would decorate it. The more detail you put in front of you the easier it is to imagine you are there. When you look at this collage of photos, you should feel the emotion as you expect to feel when you are at your completed villa. What does it look like and feel like to you?

If your vision is to be married with a family, living happily in a beautiful home, what would that look like? Find photos of homes you like, of happy healthy children, a spouse, and a car in the driveway. Use whatever images depict the feeling you want to feel. The more detail, shapes and colours you put in the pictures, the more you will begin to feel the excitement of achieving your vision.

You can also do this by creating an image on your computer so that every time you sit to work the vision comes to life on your computer screen. There are many places on the internet that allow you to build a vision board online. The key is to recreate the dream in your mind with as much detail as you can and put it on your vision board and use it to trigger your emotions.

Having order in your mind and a vision board will be very powerful in creating the life you desire. It will help you reinforce your vision and keep you focused. The more you see what you want, the harder you will work to achieve it.

It can be difficult sometimes to visualize our images. We may have had a long day and just don't want to think about things. But when you see the vision board in front of you, it forces you to bring the image in your mind, even when your will is having an off-day. It takes the struggle away and reinforces the vision for you.

When you learn to use your senses to grow your ideas, things will happen faster and more effectively for you. You will not deviate from the vision causing you to change your idea. You will stay focused and on track.

Start consciously selecting the things that are going to allow your vision to happen. If those items are not currently on your studio lot, open your gate to the studio to allow some things in to help you with your movie. Be very careful only to allow things in that will promote your vision. It is easy to get distracted with new ideas, so make sure you put what you need on your list for the gatekeeper, and only allow those items in.

You need to always be focused on your idea. All your actions should be working towards your vision. You are learning to create order in your mind and having the one idea allows you to make choices in your life to be more productive by keeping you on track for that goal.

Remember, we form impressions in our mind through our senses and they imprint into our subconscious mind. We want to let into our studio anything that will assist us in our new vision, our new movie. We are in full control of what we want to project. The more things we imprint of our new vision, the faster our projector will be running our new movie. We want something to reinforce our subconscious mind to see our vision rather than putting in the reruns.

When you look at your vision board it should trigger your emotions. It should get you excited about your idea, motivate you and make you want to put it into production!

CHAPTER 13

Your Soundtrack

Have you ever listened to a movie? Sound in movies is more intricate than you may realize. Every single sound you hear in a movie is put there intentionally. It is so controlled that even the empty sound, the ambience sound of air with no noise, is a produced sound.

The soundtrack of a movie is put there with specific triggers throughout to induce an emotion in the viewer. While we are focusing on what we see on the screen and paying attention to the dialogue, we are usually not aware of all the reactions we are having to the music and sounds that are added.

You may not consciously be hearing the sounds but your subconscious mind is absorbing every single sound and making you feel the movie. For a thriller or slasher movie, nothing makes you more nervous and on edge as the sounds of metal against metal, animals howling or loud shrieking sounds. The sound triggers you to feel the intention of the movie, to feel uncomfortable and scared. If the tone of the movie is one of serenity, perhaps a scene in a nature setting, people are relaxed and there are sounds of birds chirping, the soft cascade sound of a fountain, or children laughing in the background. These additions to movie soundtracks are to ensure that your emotions are triggered.

The main sound added to movies is music. This can be in the form of instrumental or in some cases songs with lyrics. Many movies will make their own musical scores, original productions that were created specifically for their movie. Other works use songs that are familiar to the public so they can relate to the genre or the time period of the movie.

Pay attention to the next movie you watch, and close your eyes for a minute and listen to the movie. Notice what feelings you experience while the music and sounds are playing.

Music is so powerful, it can take a room full of bored people and make them jump onto a dance floor, and it can put to sleep the most rambunctious baby.

When you hear a song on the radio, does it transport you back to a particular place and time? Can you emotionally take yourself back to an event, place or person just from hearing a song on the radio? That song played an important part because you heard it and imbedded it in your memory and tied it to that event. Perhaps you were in love with a person and that was your song. You have tied that emotion to that song. Whenever you hear it, no matter how many years have gone by, it will trigger your vision of that person and that time and place. It is one of the soundtracks in your vault that you can listen to and bring up that past movie whenever you want, where you want just by playing that song.

What I want you to do is think about the song or music that triggers a wonderful feeling in you. We all have a song that wakes us up inside, makes us want to get moving, makes us want to live. It literally wakes up an emotion inside us and makes our bodies stir. Think about that song. It may change over the years but we are all on a frequency with sound. We just need to find it. What song speaks to you?

I remember when I was a child on those hot, sunny summer days where all I did was play outside and ride my bike. My days were full of fun, playing, and going to the store to buy penny candy. I could play for hours outside with my friends from when the sun came up to when it

106

went down. The big hit at that time was "Sugar, Sugar" by the Archies. To this day, when I hear that song it takes me back to my childhood and that great happy feeling of eating candy and playing. If I want to feel happy and wake my inner child I just have to play "Sugar, Sugar." I also have songs that motivate me to move physically, drive long destinations without falling asleep, and those that wind me down from my day. The right music or song that you connect with can have a great effect on the result you want, all you have to do is listen to it to change your mood.

Another thing to think about is the lyrics in a song. A lot of songwriters are amazing story tellers and motivators, weaving their messages into their lyrics and sending us on a journey of growth. Many of these lyricists are poets and can reach us through the music as well as the words.

At this point you want to think about a piece of music or a song that gets you motivated. It can be from when you were as a child or from an exciting time or event. It needs to do one thing, and that is to set the mood for you. It must kick you into gear and motivate you towards your vision. You may want to find your motivational track that coincides with your vision. What song is your trigger? What is your soundtrack?

When you see someone jogging, chances are they have earbuds on and they are listening to something that will keep them motivated to run. They may have a song with a special beat or a sound that keeps them focused. If you want to be a long distance runner, does the Rocky Movie soundtrack get you sparked? What about building a villa in France, does French music get you in the vision? Maybe you want to attract that perfect partner and get married. Does Pachelbel's Canon in D move you? Perhaps you need something loud and electric like heavy metal to wake you up inside.

Find the songs that will trigger your body to feel the positive emotions. When you are in this positive vibration, you will be more energized and more productive. When you have these sounds, songs, or music, put them in a reel and listen to them regularly. You want to be feeling your vision on a regular basis and music is a wonderful source to keep you alive. Listen to it as often as you need to so that it will keep you in that positive state you need to be to get your results.

When you connect with the right sound you will obtain a reaction. Think about an opera singer who hits a particular high note. When she reaches it, a drinking glass matched to the exact frequency will shatter. The sound is so intense to the glass that it explodes.

Learn to use sound to keep you in a positive state and watch what comes your way. What music or sound sparks you to move into action? If a song depresses you and reminds you of the lost love that got away, or a bad time in your life, you need to stop listening to that soundtrack. Whatever your vision, there is a score for it that will shift you into gear and energize you. When you are in a good vibration you will begin to attract other individuals who feel your energy.

Like an opera singer, if you want to attract something in your life on the same frequency you need to be in the right vibration. Only then will the results be explosive!

CHAPTER 14

Setting the Stage

When you are watching a movie and are totally absorbed in a character, do you ever pay attention to the details in the room on the screen?

When you really look closely, you will see that every item in the shot serves a purpose. It is there to give you a clear description of that person's character, lifestyle, location and belongings. The set or location is meticulously designed to create the message the director wants you to receive. Every piece of furniture, flooring, curtain, or knick knack is all placed there for a reason. Nothing is an accident.

The set designer is creating a picture for you of the character so that you will be able to determine how you feel about this person. If the room is disheveled, full of garbage, used needles and empty bottles of booze, you can decipher that the character has a substance abuse problem. If the set is dressed with medals, trophies, and sports memorabilia, you know that our character is an athlete. A picture tells a thousand words and movies take advantage of this concept as much as possible. They only have a couple of hours to tell a story and the set is a great way to add detail.

In your production you need to be well aware of your surroundings. Everything on your set should serve a purpose and represent something to support your vision.

Many actors before shooting will visit the set and walk through it in advance to get familiar with the surroundings. If they can touch and feel the items in the room, their action will be more natural.

You are currently on a set that you could probably walk around with your eyes closed. You are doing things without even thinking. You know the routine, you know the process and you can play your part like second nature. What we are doing, however, is creating a new set that subconscious mind is not going to know. It's like introducing a new piece of furniture in your room. For the first while, you bump into it a lot until you become conditioned to know it's there.

In order for your subconscious mind to receive the message loud and clear about your new goal, the more clues we can send about what it looks and feels like, the better. In creating your vision you want to have as much of your set as you can to reinforce it to your subconscious mind. The best place for you to start creating a set for your vision is with what you have now.

The first thing you must do is create the space for it. This seems so logical to do when we know something is being delivered. For example, when you order a new sofa, you remove the old sofa by either discarding or selling it, then you make space for the new one. We know the delivery date in advance and we plan to have the spot ready for it. Planning for the delivery of something when you know the date is quite simple. But planning for the delivery of something without knowing when it will be delivered takes a little more work.

As you complete your vision and are clear about what it is you want, you need to have faith in knowing that it will come. You need to believe that the delivery is on its way, your vision is in transit, but the only difference is that you have no tracking information. Creating the space for what you are bringing into your life is a reminder for you that it is on its way and will keep you focused on your goal.

Let's take for example the individual whose dream it is to be a concert pianist. They have always loved music and they want to play and teach piano to other people. The problem is that they don't own a piano. Their current environment is the result of their past thinking and they are now creating a new vision, a new movie, and this particular shot needs a piano. If their vision is to be playing a piano, they have to have a piano to complete the set design.

There are a few things that can be done to complete this process in their current environment. They can start by making the space in the current home for the new piano. This will help prepare for the delivery and every time they walk by the spot they can picture the piano there and know that it's coming. They are convincing their subconscious mind that they are a piano owner.

To take this visual even further, they can visit a piano dealer, be seated at various pianos and play them. They would feel the piano keys and envision themselves playing at home in their designated spot. Finally, they can take home some brochures of various pianos to help keep the vision alive in their minds.

The key is to trick your subconscious mind that you are a pianist. When you have faith that the item is coming it will be delivered. The true proof of belief is when you make the space for the item. This will stir up the emotion inside you and will create that energy you need to emit to attract your vision.

There is a famous quote from the movie Field of Dreams, "If you build it, they will come." This movie took "having faith" to the extreme.

Kevin Costner plays a farmer on the brink of bankruptcy, who in the middle of his corn fields, hears a voice telling him to build a baseball field. Not knowing why he is being led to do this, but trusting his instinct, he listens to the voice and begins to destroy his only means of income, his corn fields. He builds a baseball field risking his livelihood and becomes the laughing stock of his town. He put all his efforts into this vision, and even with all the opposition he stays true to his commitment and completes the field. In the end we discover why he had to build the field and he solves his financial crisis, all because he did not deviate from his goal. This movie was a bit on the extreme side of creating your dream but the point is true. You need to believe in you and your goal and stay focused on it no matter what the circumstances.

When you create space for something, and you believe it will be delivered, it sets in motion a movement to make it come to fruition.

Now what if your vision requires you to be somewhere other than where you are now? How do you convince your subconscious mind that you will be on location in another city or country? How can you continue to project your vision to your subconscious mind through your senses with a set that you don't have yet?

You can do this without having the actual location but something similar. Remember the subconscious does not know the difference between fact and fiction. For example, if your dream is to have a home that overlooks the ocean, you don't need to visit the actual home on the ocean. You can go to a beach and pretend you are in your home on the beach and feel the emotions of owing a house on the beach. Just like in the movies, they don't always go to actual locations. They make you believe you are on location. You just need to put yourself in a position where you have the point of view as if you are looking at the same result as you have in your vision.

The movie industry tricks us into believing locations all the time, sometimes just by changing the signs on the street. If they are in San Francisco and want you to believe they are in Italy, they just change the sign to an Italian city name. They do not go to Italy to get the shot. You can be in a downtown street right now in the middle of your city and do the same thing. Your subconscious mind won't know the difference.

If your dream is to move to Paris and become a chef, visit a French restaurant in your area. Go to a French movie or visit a bakery that sells French pastries. Sign up for French lessons in your area and speak French to yourself and to others. Your mind will not know the difference. Just change the signs.

The signals that you send to your subconscious mind are what are important. Just like in a movie, we want it to believe we are in a certain place. It will not know the difference. It's not what's happening around you that is important, it is what your subconscious mind believes. And the way to put it in action is to feel the emotion.

The more you can demonstrate to your subconscious mind the vision that you want to obtain, the faster it will make it a habit and put into action the results you want.

CHAPTER 15

The Casting Call

In the film industry, when a script is finalized, agents are given the task of finding the right actors to play the parts in the movie. They are given a sheet with the specs of exactly the parts that are available and the type of person they want to play them. Directors then hold a Casting Call where agents send the most suitable actors to audition for the roles.

The good news for you is that you already have the lead in this movie. The part has been written just for you and you get to play it as yourself. This is great at this point if your vision is a one-person show. But what if there are other people you want involved? Do you see a supporting cast in your movie?

Are you looking for an ideal partner, or maybe an assistant or group of people to work with you in your new role? Who are they and what parts will they be playing?

Adding people to your vision gets a little more interesting. Remember, just like you, we all want to be the stars in our own movie. People have their own genre, their own scripts, and they may not be a match to yours.

When we are truly clear on what our vision is and what our movie is about, we need to decide how much we are willing to let go of to allow someone else in. Others may want to influence you with their ideas and to change your script a bit to suit them. Are you willing to compromise?

When things get difficult in our lives, our subconscious mind starts telling us that we are too demanding, we are selfish and to stop asking for so much. Remember, we have reruns that are waiting to be played and would make things much easier. Sometimes, it seems easier to compromise than to face the uncomfortable feeling of standing up for ourselves and going after what we truly want.

How clear are you on your role in your vision and what you are willing to allow into it?

If your vision is to see yourself living on a boat sailing the seas with the love of your life, and you meet someone who hates being out on the water, will you be willing to compromise? Or, will you force your vision on that person and make them conform to yours? How fair would that be to the other person? What if you find that perfect job, with great pay, but your morals and ethics are tested? Are you willing to throw your dreams away for the sake of someone else's belief?

We know that if we keep our natural forces from expression, we bottle up the feelings and it eventually releases itself in a negative manner. It's important that we are all free to be who we really are meant to be, but also to be aware of the expression of others around us. It's a wonderful thing when you can achieve your vision with the support of others where they don't have to pay a price.

Not long ago, movie studios used to "own" their actors and actresses. They were basically commodities in a multimillion dollar industry, and were bought and sold by the studios. Many actresses blinded by their hopes of stardom flocked to Hollywood to try out for parts in the hopes they would be the next star in a production.

Unfortunately, some studio people abused this power with the starlets. These women would audition for the roles and then would be asked to prove their worth on the "casting couch." Many women moved from the couch to stardom, but many more did not. They were willing to give up their morals and standards to pursue their dreams and in the end they failed. They were taken advantage of by people that saw their vulnerability and preyed on them.

Many of these women did move on in their careers by "performing" their auditions on the couch, but they were also playing a part in some else's script even if they didn't believe in it. They just wanted to be in the movies so badly they would do anything. We can say that their dreams of being stars came true, but the road to getting there wasn't as they had planned.

This is a very important point to understand about you and other people. Whoever you are currently seeking is also seeking you! You get delivered exactly what you ask for and if you are not clear enough it may come to you in the wrong way. These women did not clarify their goals enough. They should have had their goal so well defined that they did nothing illegal or immoral to become a star. Then, when their dream was achieved, it was earned and appreciated with no regrets.

The thing you need to notice at this point is that you are going to be opening your gate to allow people into your studio lot. Who do you want to let in? If you want to have other people in your dream, you need to make this so clear that the supporting cast is there by their choice because they share the same vision with you. You do not impose yourself onto other people. You must be all interested in the same vision and share the same goals. Your director, or in this case your will should not impose on another person's will. They may conform for a while but they will eventually walk off the set because they don't feel the part. They will want you to change your script.

When a studio is preparing to make a movie, they interview people based on who they see playing the part in the movie. Who do you need to allow into your studio to perform this new vision? If you see yourself with a spouse, happily married and with children, what does this person look and act like? Are they tall or short, man or woman, shy or dominant? Just like with a part in a movie, you cannot expect an agent to send you the talent if you do not tell them for what you are looking. It is time to take your imagination another step and focus on the details of who you want in your life.

If you want to be a singer, are you a solo artist? Are you part of a band or are they just backup singers? What instruments are they playing? How many of them are there? Are you singing in a lounge with just a piano player or are you on a huge stage with an orchestra? Be very clear of what you expect to come to fruition. You can see the confusion you can cause if you are not clear on this one point.

What people do you want to attract? If you are crystal clear on this point you will be able to find them and they will find you. If you are a businessperson, are you alone in a small office with just an assistant? Do you have a team of managers under your direction? What does your staff look like? How many people do you lead? Just answering these questions can help you focus on the things you need to look at like the size of office space you will need, the salaries you will be paying, the income you will be earning. Finding a personal assistant is a lot different than attracting high paid executives to run your company. Be very clear on the type of individuals you want on your call sheet.

If you are on a beach, sipping a drink, who is sitting next to you? Are there children playing around you? Who is serving you the drink? This vision alone can be unclear because you can be living on a friend's couch and be dead broke and still have these results. If it is a spouse you want

118

to attract for your beach home then you need to send out the call sheet for someone who loves the ocean. Be as clear as possible. You do not want anything to stop you from attaining your dream.

You have been doing things a certain way for a long time. You have a rerun going through your vault showing you who and what to bring into your life. Your first reaction is to bring in the same things and people you have always done before.

If you have been attracting a certain type of individual in your life in the past, and you want to change that, you need to make up a new list of items on your call sheet to attract that supporting actor. If you have been surrounded by serious people but you want someone with a sense of humour, then put that on your list of demands. This is a made-to-order part.

If you are a woman who always attracts men who treat you badly, you need to put on your call sheet exactly how you want this new man to act and treat you. If you want a man to respect you, then the order sheet for the casting call will have "respectful" on the order.

There is a scene in the movie "Paradise" that starred Melanie Griffin and Don Johnson. She and her husband have had a tumultuous relationship and she is telling the story of how they met to a young child. She describes how she was the instigator in the relationship by approaching her future husband and saying, "You look like trouble, want to take me out?" It's no wonder she is in a troubled relationship, she ordered it.

What are your past behaviours? Have you been attracting the same type of person in your life and getting the same bad results? If you want to change the results, you need to be absolutely clear who you want around you.

You have implanted the thoughts from your previous thinking into your subconscious mind and have put them into production to obtain the results you currently have in your life. To change the results, you need to change the image of the supporting cast.

When you start meeting people who are auditioning for the part in your movie, what will you do if they are missing something on your list? Will you walk them off the set? Are you willing to compromise your dream or stick to the script and be patient until the right actor comes and auditions for your supporting part?

Many of us go through life thinking that there is no one perfect for the role we have imagined so we settle for whoever is willing to take the part. We start justifying our vision that we were too demanding and we change our script to conform to another person's ideas. When the script gets adjusted to conform to another actor's vision, things get disrupted, and the original intention of the movie may get lost. You start making a new movie and your original script dies.

Your director needs to have a clear vision of what you want in order to keep what you don't want out of the lot. If your director has a clear outline, a detailed spec sheet, you are going to be letting people through your gate who fill the part exactly according to plan.

You are not doing the things you did before. Who and what you allow into your lot is going affect your production. Have faith that there is a perfect actor for every part and know that they will be auditioning. Keep your faith alive and learn to be patient. If you are true to yourself and in the right vibration, you will attract exactly what meets your criteria. Know that what you are seeking is currently seeking you.

CHAPTER 16

Staying in Character

One of the most entertaining things I have ever seen in the movie industry is those Asian kung fu movies where the actors have had their voices dubbed in English. They usually consist of a man in an action sequence, kicking and jumping and clearly out of breath, and his mouth is moving not only out of sync to the sound, but the voice is coming out monotone and in English. The mood and the words do not match the action of the actor.

I'm sure in their real language these movies were exciting and popular, which is why they made their way to the Americas. How disheartening it must have been for those actors and directors who put so much emphasis on a serious and dramatic movie to be shown as comedic and ridiculous to the viewers when translated.

I want to use this example to show you that what we are thinking and what we say do not always get delivered in the manner we had hoped. Remember, your subconscious mind is delivering your actions to your body, not your conscious mind. Until your subconscious mind believes in the new action, it will not see that it is put into effect.

You need to understand the importance of your attitude and how it affects your results. What you think about causes how you feel and that feeling gets shown through your body. Just like a dubbed movie, you can be saying one thing, but the message being sent out is very different.

When we send out an unintended message, we get disheartened and do not understand why our results are the opposite of what we intended. We start off making our serious kung fu action movie and we end up with an audience laughing. What went wrong?

If I am thinking negative thoughts about a person, but I smile and tell them that I love them, they will sense that I am not sincere about my message. When your actions do not match your emotions it is obvious and comes across as confusing.

You need to be aware of your attitude and what message you are sending. Until you are aligned and you begin to have faith and belief in your thought, your body will not be projecting the action to others the way you intended. The message being sent is deceptive.

A similar effect happens in the movie industry. Imagine you are watching a scene where an actor is smoking a cigarette. Up and down his hand goes while he takes a puff and in our minds we register that he is smoking. But what if every time he brought his hand up, the length of the cigarette changed? What if the cigarette was short, then the next time it came up it was long, and then it was short again?

These errors happen in movies all the time and we usually don't notice them but our subconscious mind sees them loud and clear. For some reason we just don't buy into the movie. We can't put our finger on it, but we just don't relate to the character. We do not believe in the character and do not have the feeling intended from the scene.

This is a crucial process in the movie industry. Most movies are shot out of sequence, using one set, rearranging it to represent different scenes in the movie. Sometimes it is shot from different angles on different days.

It is the job of the "continuity" person to ensure that everything is in its place and where it should be, from shot to shot. They may take photos of the area to ensure when they come back everything is where they left it and they can refer to the photos for reference. The goal is that the scene is created and performed with a constant flow so that we believe it is happening in real time.

It is important that when a scene is shot several times that we are seeing everything as it's happening in order. If we do not see everything in sync we feel a different message than what was intended.

You need to be aware of continuity in your part as well. If you want to become a certain person and act a particular way, you need to be continuous in your belief and your manner.

If you are acting a part of a certain person but don't believe it, you're sending out a different message and people will feel this and not trust you. If you are a salesperson that does not believe in your product, and you shake a prospects hand, you may be saying "nice to meet you" but the energy you are sending is "don't buy this product." You will be losing sales and not know why. Even though you are using all of the sales techniques you were taught, because your belief is negative, your body is going to send out that message. And this is really dangerous if the product you are marketing is you! If you do not believe in yourself, no one else will either.

A few years ago I saw a movie by Albert Brooks called "Mother." It is the perfect example of how powerful your attitude is and how it can affect your results.

Debbie Reynolds plays the part of a mother of two sons played by Albert Brooks (John) and Rob Morrow (Jeff). John is a science fiction writer who is just ending his second marriage. He has come to the realization that the problems he is facing with women stem from the fact that his mother never loved him like she loved Jeff. He feels she does not accept that he is a writer and that she resents him and in turn this is causing him to attract women who resent him as well.

The mother, who clearly is attached to the son Jeff, denies the allegations and believes John is confused. She continues to defend her position that she loves both sons equally but it is very clear through her actions that she is more distant with John. John decides the best way to get to the bottom of this problem is for him to move in with his mother, and rekindle their relationship to discover the truth behind her resentment.

The movie is very entertaining as John returns to the childhood home and redecorates his old room exactly as it was before he moved out. Eventually, John and his mother begin to bond, talk about personal issues and they get to the root of their relationship.

We discover that John's mother was a writer before she married his dad. Not only did the arrival of John take her away from her writing, but when he grew up he became a published author, something she always dreamed for herself. Even though she loved her sons and never thought there were any issues, her true feelings of resentment were being transmitted to John through her actions. John could feel this negative energy in everything she would say or do with him. The mother was unintentionally sending the message to John that she was jealous because he was living her dream.

This is how powerful your attitude can become and how it can take control of your results.

When you go against your natural energy, it is like filming in the dark, and people will perceive you are unclear, deceptive or have ulterior motives.

The great thing is that to adjust your attitude, all you have to do is adjust your thoughts. Rethink your attitude. Sometimes it just requires making small changes in your life.

In the movie "Mother", Debbie Reynolds begins to write again and takes back control of her original dream. You too can do things to make changes and take back your control. You first need to know what result you want.

The interesting thing is that when you learn to change your attitude in one aspect of your life, it will affect everything in your life. You are creating a new way of living your life, just like creating a movie, so it only makes sense to do what the movie studios do to get their completed shots.

When filming is done on a scene and the actor makes a mistake or the take just doesn't seem right, they cut the film and start over again. At the end of the day of filming, directors will look at the shots to make sure they captured everything they needed before moving on to the next scene. These views are called the "dailies." If there is a problem, they go back and redo it until they get their final shot. You can do the same thing.

When doing your new movie you're going to run into obstacles. You're not going to get the result you want with your first take. You need to redo it again and again until you get the shot.

What happens with most people is that they go in with an attitude, do not get the results and feel that they cannot get their message across. They decide that they are not capable, quit and walk away from the situation.

When things don't go as planned, just rethink your thought. Check your dailies and review what went wrong and decide that you will do it again but better. You need to get in sync with who you want to be and ensure you're living that part in everything you do.

For example, if you are a person that is reactive and easily gets upset, and your vision is to be a patient and understanding parent, then your thoughts should begin with you seeing yourself as a patient and understanding person. How you do one thing is how you do everything so if you can create patience and understanding in one area of your life it will recreate in others as well.

Remember, you are trying to change a pattern that has become entrenched in your subconscious mind all your life. Your old movie may have been to always react by yelling and screaming. This may take some time to change. The key is to stay on the set and continue with the process. Eventually the new thought pattern will be impressed and come through in everything you do.

If on one particular occasion you yelled and lost your temper and went totally against your vision, go back and review your dailies. At some point you must have changed your attitude and told yourself you were not patient and understanding and you changed your character somewhere for you to lose your cool. Find out what triggered you to act the way you did in that particular situation. Sometimes we can locate a pattern that changes our behavior.

Know that you can start over again, refocus and adjust your take, and become your role again and relive it as if it went according to plan. Realize where you went wrong and practice changing the behavior. Keep in character and remember to be in a continuous movement. The more you rehearse, the better you will play your part.

Introduce patience and understanding in other areas of your life gradually as well. If you are commuting to work on a daily basis and are constantly frustrated by the traffic, people cutting you off, and the long line ups at lights, think

126

of how you can apply patience and understanding into your commute. Change the way you think.

Instead of yelling and honking when someone goes to budge in front of you, decide that perhaps they have a sick parent they are trying to get to or their child is sick and they need to get them to the doctor. When you feel yourself getting emotional about a situation, turn it into an event where you need to draw patience and understanding.

I practiced this when my commute was an hour and half each way every day. What I did to survive was to make a game with my fellow commuters. I would decide every morning that I had to allow no less than three cars to go in ahead of me on the way to work and the way home. What happened was surprising. Not only did I feel more relaxed and less stressed when I got to work, I was greeted by happy drivers with wonderful smiles and waves as they appreciated my kindness in helping them with their commute. By changing my attitude about my commute I changed my results. I would arrive at work in a much better mood and my patience in other areas of my life grew as well.

When you go in with the wrong attitude and you get a negative reaction, just know that you can always do another take. After all, you are human and you are going to make mistakes. You are learning a new behavior.

You are the only one responsible for your results and need to understand how important it is to stay in character. When you believe in your part and stick to the script you will eventually become that person in everything you do as the new character emerges.

When you are on track with your attitude, there is an underlying intensity that you emit as you become energized. You will feel it with your results. Everything that happens to you is a reflection of your current attitude. Be clear on the message you want to send and there will be no misinterpretation. You will know because the reactions and results that you are expecting will be delivered.

CHAPTER 17

The Art of Editing

There is a common phrase you may have heard in the film industry when something goes wrong in filming. They say, "Don't worry, we'll fix it in post." What they are referring to is post production. This is the part of the movie-making process where, once all of the images, sounds and items are finalized and catalogued, they are all compiled and pieced together to make the movie. This is truly where the "magic" of movie-making happens and the magician who orchestrates the putting together of the pieces is the film editor. This person is usually locked away in a room for weeks, with a pot of coffee, stale food and lots of Tylenol.

Every item that was made for the movie is labeled and tagged with the information of when it was shot, where it was shot, and where it's intended to go in the movie. The editor then takes every shot, frame by frame, and pieces it together to form the final product, and has the ability to alter the image's color, size, motion, or formatting in order to capture the mood or feeling of the movie.

Years ago when movies were shot on film the task of editing was literally done by hand. Miles of film were labeled and sent to the editor and they would go through each piece of film, decide what was not going to be used, then splice it off with a cutter. The discarded pieces would land on the floor and end up in the trash. Many actors spent a lot of their time and effort acting in a film, only to find out later their only scene ended up on the "cutting room floor."

Today most movies are done digitally and the cutting is done on the computer. Not as messy but just as traumatic to an actor.

At this point you are probably thinking that being an editor should be easy. They just take the pieces of the puzzle and put them all together, right? Well, that's not the case.

The editor, with the assistance of the director, will manipulate all information in a way that it will capture the essence of the message they want to deliver to the audience. It isn't just important that they show you the shots, it is how the shots are shown to you. The order and the way they are put together can change the meaning enormously. Depending on the result the director wants, the events are carefully planned and executed.

For example, I want you to imagine that there is a shot of a man entering a building, we see him walking up the stairs, he continues down the hall, and then we see a close-up of his hand opening his office door. Now there is another shot of the office and under the desk there is a bomb on the floor and we see that the fuse is lit. The shot is one minute of the fuse as it burns down and then the bomb blows up.

If we are making an action movie we want to build the excitement gradually so that we get the true effect of the movie. We want it to ignite our emotions. The way we just shot it does not do that. It is giving us the message but we have no feelings.

This is where the editor comes in.

Now imagine the story with added music, sound effects and the editor manipulating the information.

We see the man entering the building and the music may be a little carefree. We now cut to the lit bomb and the music changes to be a little more dramatic. You now see the danger. What was a carefree scene is now more suspenseful. Is he going to the office with the bomb?

We cut back to the man walking up the stairs and the music gets a little more suspenseful as the shots cut back to the bomb fuse starting to burn. Is the bomb in his office?

It then cuts to the man walking down the hall coming closer to the office, we see the bomb again with the fuse burned closer to the end, we then see his hand reaching for the door knob, the music is louder, more suspenseful, we go back to the fuse and see it at the end, and then?

Note the difference.

Did the cause of the sequence of events change the reaction you had to the scene?

The editor of a movie has the power to create whatever feeling they want the viewer to resonate by adding and taking out the things that do not serve the final outcome.

They take care and attention to every detail to ensure what they want in the end happens. They are clear on what needs to be in full view to get the reaction. They also did not use lots of shots of the man walking in the hallway that did not serve the purpose of completing the scene. Those clips are all taken out and the main ones are left in to complete the sequence of events.

You, much like an editor, have been compiling scenes all your life and you need to decide what needs to be included to make your movie happen and more importantly what clips do not serve a purpose. What sequences are in your life right now, that need to be spliced and dropped to the cutting room floor, and what things should be inserted to make your dream a reality? It is important to plan out your movie.

Let's start by locating the things that need to be cut from your current life. If you currently have a habit or behavior that you want to omit, something you are doing that does not support your goal, try not to focus so much on what you are doing, but what is triggering you to do the behavior. Every effect that is in your current environment was brought on by a cause. If you find the cause you can change the effect.

An example would be the vision of being a certain weight and leading a healthy life. Every morning however for the past year you are in a hurry for work so you go to the drive-through and pick up breakfast. You always say you are going to order the light meal but once there, you order the one with high fat and calories. The temptation was just too strong to say no.

The way to remove this scene from your life is to take the action away, cutting the driving by the restaurant all together. If you don't go there, there will be no temptation. If you begin driving a different street, where you will not be faced with the temptation, this can be a start to changing your habit. The overeating isn't the issue in this action, it's putting yourself in a situation where you will be tempted. Take away the temptation and it becomes easier.

Pack some items in your car so that if you do have the urge, you can eat something right away. Set some time every week where you make breakfast packages that are in the fridge so that you can grab and go. Whatever the scene, replace it with one that conforms to your purpose. Change it to a scene that will get you emotionally charged about your goal.

You need to start sorting through your daily actions and deciding which ones do not serve you. Once you find them, you can either replace them with a new scene, or cut them out all together.

You are not able to change things unless you are aware of them. Really pay attention to your behavior. How are you reacting to certain things in your life? When you react, look at what triggered you. Now you can start editing. What things are you currently doing that are not going to support your goal? Anything that does not apply or does not contribute to your final outcome needs to end up on the cutting room floor.

When you are clear what you want, you know what to keep and what not to keep. Whatever you choose to leave in your film ultimately will have an effect on the movie. This is the magic of your movie, as you are in full control to make whatever scene you want to see in your projector.

You are changing a habit and this takes a lot of focus and attention that is why like a movie an editor usually only works on one project at a time. It would be in your best interest as well to focus on only one vision at a time for this same reason.

Remember, every habit that you currently have in your life will not leave you. It is in your vault. The only thing you can do is decide whether to watch the rerun over and over or move it to the back of the vault and replace it with the new movie.

My best example for someone transforming to obtain what they want has to be the movie "Grease." John Travolta plays Danny Zuko, the cool, leather jacket-toting gang member who spends all his time smoking, carousing and stealing hub caps. Danny then meets the subdued, straight-as-an-arrow Sandy, who does not smoke or drink, and finds Danny to be rather immature. She turns her affections to an educated football star and athlete, leaving Danny heartbroken.

Danny, deciding that his vision is to win Sandy over, puts into action a sequence of events that will cause his dream to happen. He stops spending time driving around with his buddies and instead joins the track team at school. He runs

133

with the team and concentrates on his schoolwork and then graduates at the end of the year with a letterman sweater, all in the hopes of attracting the affections of Sandy. He edited everything in his life that didn't serve him, including cutting out his friends, and only focused on the things that would promote his winning Sandy.

When you put your plan into effect, things will start changing for you. You want to spend your time only on the things that will get your movie completed. In others words, what do you need to be doing to make your dream come true?

Just as important as cutting things from your life, you also need to know what to add to make the scene come alive. What will support you to make that emotion of the vision come to the surface?

Just like adding the sound effects and music bring the vision alive, what do you need to add that will create the effect you want? If your goal requires some sort of education or research for you to complete the vision, start thinking about those things you can add to your day to lead you on the path of success.

We know that the gate to your studio has been wide open and you have been allowing things into your life that do you disservice. When you are focused, you start letting in things that serve a purpose.

It's time to take control of your production and what you allow into your studio lot. Take stock in what you spend your time on and what can you replace it with to move you forward into the direction of your goal.

Editing, much like the creation of your vision, is a process. It is time-consuming and requires a lot of focus and attention. The more time you spend on the details, the bigger and better your production will be. When you put all your energy into one idea, it has no choice but to grow. You will eventually be spending your time editing until you achieve your goal-your finished product.

THE

FEATURE

PRESENTATION

Releasing Your Vision

The Movie Trailer

CHAPTER 18

Facing the Critics

With every movie script, what moves the action from one scene to another and keeps our interest is making things go from the positive to the negative. Something good happens with our hero and we are excited for them but then out of nowhere, something bad happens and they are challenged. If we didn't have this in the movie, the story would be in one constant state of emotion and we would get bored.

Staying true to life, for every movie that has a protagonist, there is an antagonist not too far away ready to oppose the hero and do everything in their power to stop them from achieving their goal. The decisions and the will of the hero to win usually determine the outcome of the movie. How strongly will the protagonist fight to the finish and will they overcome the antagonist?

It goes without saying that whenever you do good and cause some change you are going to be up against someone who does not like or agree with what you are doing.

As you put your new vision in your projector, with every thought that you implant into your subconscious mind a new energy is being formed and that image will have a different vibration.   That energy can be felt by all those around you.

The interesting thing about this new energy is that it may feel absolutely amazing, you may be flying high, and you will start doing things and talking about things you never talked about before. Your thoughts may change from negative to positive and your sedate life may turn into an active life. You will begin to change.

The problem with this new-felt energy is that you are currently surrounded by people, places and things from your past thinking. Your current persona and environment are there now in front of you. Every person around you now is playing the supporting role in your past movie and you are asking them to support a new star.

As your vibration changes, those around you are going to feel it. Those closest to you will sense it and this will either repel or attract them.

Unfortunately, the first people to view the changes in your current performance are going to be those closest to you, your friends and family. You were part of their movie as a supporting cast member but now you are trying to step onto their stage and make them the supporting cast.

Your new performance may not be well received and you need to be prepared for the critics. You responded to certain cues and acted a certain role and the people around you expect the same performance. If you step out with new lines and a new script, they may not recognize you and they are going to react.

Understand that these people not only care about you but also believe they know what's best for you, even if you feel differently. They are comfortable with you the way you are, with the same energy and responses they are used to seeing. They like that you are always a certain way and they have adapted to that feeling.

When you share your vision with other people, they may not agree with you. They may tell you that you are crazy, a dreamer, that it is impossible. This is because they have their own interpretations and cannot possibly understand what you are thinking. No one but you can see your vision. There is no way you can expect someone else to see it. The only way another person can see your vision is if you complete it and show it to them.

It's hard enough that you are constantly dealing with your own mind issues, the antagonists are going to suddenly make an appearance around you as well.

There are a couple of things that you need to understand when you are changing your vision and your vibration.

If you know that you are going to be facing criticism, the best thing you can do is be prepared for it. Remember, you cannot change others, only yourself, but you can change the way you react to them. It's not your responsibility to make others accept you in your role. Do not stop your performance because of someone's judgment. If this were the case there would be no standup comedians in the world. These are professionals who truly know how to deal with backlash from people.

In their case they have to deal with the dreaded "heckler" during their performances. These individuals are usually drunk, silly or just want attention. Comedians know that the possibility of a heckler could arise so they come prepared to deal with them. They may have an arsenal of one-liners to throw back, they may ignore them, or better yet, just have them removed from the audience. But it wouldn't make sense that a comedian would quit being a standup because of what a heckler shouted at them.

The key here is that the comedian understands that hecklers are dealing with their own issues, their own insecurities and the heckling has absolutely nothing to do with the comedian personally.

The same can be said about critics who are going to have opinions about your performance. You must remember that this is just an opinion. You are creating a new character, a new performance, and some people will need time to adjust.

It's like when you first see a shining, bright light. You are now a lot brighter than you were before, with new energy passing through you and people need time to adjust. Just like our pupils need time to adjust when we step out from the dark into the light, at first it is uncomfortable until our eyes focus. Those closest to you need time to adjust the focus on their lenses. Many are happy that you want to be the star of your production, but you changed the lighting on the set. At first they may turn away, but eventually they will be able to step into the brightness that you will be emitting.

Most of the time people do eventually come along for the ride with you, especially when they see the positive changes happening. It's important to always focus on your behavior and allow others to adapt to you rather than forcing a change in them.

But the most important thing to notice with your new vision is to understand the difference between criticism and collaboration.

As you are releasing your vision and beginning to attract some amazing things into your life, it will be affecting those around you. There will be many opinions, many criticisms towards you but there may also be many suggestions that will help you move ahead in your goal.

If you are constantly in a defensive mode, you may miss out on some information that will be beneficial for you in achieving your success. Many people go into their performance with blinders on and keep everyone and everything away from them while they perform. They want no distractions while they focus on their vision. This is a great thing but it may also close out some people and ideas that may be beneficial to you. Understand that sometimes what you hear as criticism is actually collaboration.

When you share your idea with someone and then they change your idea by adding something different to the original, they are telling you that they have accepted your idea and understand what you are doing, and they're excited about it and adding the vision of how they perceive it to be.

The usual response for someone totally focused is to defend their original idea and take the comment as the person is trying to change the vision.

At this point, it is not the person that is a problem for you, it's how you choose to react to them. These people get what you are doing, they are just adding their spin to it. There is no need to defend anything.

This is an important concept to understand if you are used to reacting a certain way. You may be creating more problems than you think. We need to understand when we are reacting to criticism based on our performance, rather than personally.

If you take any criticism as a personal attack on your person, you may be missing opportunities that will move you ahead in your performance. When someone sees your potential and gives you advice, don't block this attempt at collaboration by taking it as an attack on your person. Know that this may be something from another movie in your vault. You may be using a rerun as a way to react.

Have you ever had a great idea and shared it with four or five people, maybe your friends, or in a boardroom meeting? You are so excited that you came up with this idea and everyone agreed it was great, but then someone made a suggestion on how to improve it.

Did you take it personally and want to defend your idea or did you listen attentively, understand their position and how it might be beneficial, and then respond to it objectively?

In no way do you have to accept the suggestions if you are firm on the idea, but you need to see the difference between someone who thinks your idea is terrible and dismisses it with another person who agrees with your idea but just has a different take on it. We are all different and have different points of view. No one will ever see things exactly the way you do.

This is similar to brainstorming. Maybe the idea they are offering is putting you both on the same level of understanding and building rapport between you. Learn to look at everything that is said to you with different eyes. These people, no matter what they are telling you, may be offering something to help you improve. When you open yourself to hearing them rather than reacting to them, this is a freeing experience. You get to be who you want to be and at the same time allow others to share.

Hear the message as them collaborating with you. This takes some practice but after a while there will be more harmony in your life because the other individual feels you have accepted them.

Sometimes severe changes affect those around us because they are closest to us and are used to things being a certain way.

For example, you have jet black hair but you always wanted to be a blond. You go to the salon and spend hundreds of dollars and come out as the new you, looking and feeling like a million bucks. You are finally the person you always wanted to be with blond hair and you look fabulous! Everyone in the salon is complimenting you and you get a few looks of approval from strangers on the street. You wonder why you didn't do this sooner.

You go home with your new blond hair ready to get the same reactions you had at the salon. You walk in smiling and happy, only to be confronted with gasps and laughter at your new look. The comments you get are even more offensive, including that you look terrible as a blond, you must have been out of your mind and that you should go back to your original jetblack colour.

Everyone at your work and home are shocked at your new look and you feel terrible. Your first reaction is to hide your hair, go back to the salon and return to your natural jet black colour. How could you have been so stupid to think you looked good as a blond?

At this point, you may start the back-talk and justify why your family and friends are right. In fact, you may go so far as to think everyone in the salon was in on it, and they just wanted your money. After all, why would they care what you looked like? You chalk it up to a crazy whim that you had and you go back to your regular colour.

Instead of taking it so personally, listen to what they are saying. Maybe it isn't that you look terrible as a blond, but that the blond hair looks terrible in their eyes because they are used to seeing you with black hair. It isn't the colour that is bad it is the reaction that is making them feel bad. Understand that you had time to adjust to the new you, give others time as well.

How many of us can relate to this situation? I remember the first time I saw Julia Roberts with a short pixie cut for the movie Hook. I wasn't ready for the look as I always saw her as a long-haired brunette. But it worked in the movie and I just had to see her objectively for her performance in Hook. The same can be said about an actor that you regularly see playing in comedies and now you see them in a drama. At first we don't want to accept it but once we see the finished product we see things differently.

When you are in your new vision, you are acting a new part and you have to be ready all the time to react to things that will go wrong on the set. A true professional always stays in character.

When you begin to feel the excitement coming through you in your new role, it is that energy that you want to hold on to all the time. Let it flow through you with full force. It may literally "shock" people and knock some over with your new electricity, but you need to release it.

When you take the point of view that people are not criticizing but collaborating with you it can change the way you react. Exude your light and be that shining star. You don't need the spotlight of other people on you to perform because you are lighting up the stage with what is burning inside you. When you shine brightly, others will want to come out of the dark and be part of your light. People will be around you and want to be a part of it because it feels good just to be near you.

Your family and your friends are the most important people in your life. You will be affecting them as you grow. Be patient. When you are in the performance and you are sending out that light, your family and friends are the ones who eventually will be in the front row.

CHAPTER 19

Receiving Awards

When you start acting on your vision, you are likely expecting the negative things that will be coming your way, the obstacles you will be facing, and how you may want to deal with them. But have you thought about how you are going to react when something good comes your way?

You may think that this thought is ridiculous, but in reality you are probably more likely to accept the negative things that will come to you before you accept the positive.

Why would anyone refuse a good response to what they're working towards?

Remember, you may still be operating on old movies, reruns that are affecting everything you currently do and what you currently have in your life. In order to change you have to be aware that many of things you have programmed in you are out of your control. You are doing them without even knowing. Your subconscious mind is in control and if it believes you are not worthy to receive, it will deliver that message through your actions.

Until you believe you are worthy of receiving the gifts, the money, the fame, or the success, you may be your own worst enemy. You will sabotage your own acceptance of these things.

You may think you are ready for the applause, the awards and the accolades of your new position, but the fact is, we usually don't know where we stand until we're put in the position to receive.

How worthy are you?

You can do everything this book has prompted you to do, and your vision, your success, money or partners can begin to be delivered to you. But if you do not know how to receive them, all the work you have done will be fruitless.

You must break the cycle of unworthiness, and change it to the belief that you deserve everything you attract. If you see yourself as your rerun, it will ensure that you will stay in that position. If you are not ready to receive, you cannot accept what is given to you no matter how hard it is thrown at you.

When the universe begins to deliver what you are attracting, you are not going to notice, because you have been watching for different outcomes. Many of us were raised with the notion that money and power are a sign of greed and that to obtain it we must have been underhanded or evil. If you have this idea in your subconscious mind, when you receive money or power you are going to repel it. You will tell yourself that you are not worthy of it and sabotage your own success.

Your mindset needs to be one that is accepting all that is given to you so that you can receive it and realize your vision. You are deserving of everything you are going to achieve. The idea that needs to be reinforced is that the energy you are putting out into your new idea has to come back to you somehow, in the form of money, success, or in other ways to achieve your goal. It is a universal law. What you put out is what you will get back.

Pay attention to the signals and the opportunities that are coming around you all of a sudden. Your old way of thinking may have you pass up on things that are intended for you to receive them.

Have you ever encountered an attractive, successful person and decided that they are too good for you so you avoided meeting them? How many jobs did you not apply for because you decided you weren't good enough and you

148

were intimidated by the size or stature of the company? Think about how many opportunities you have passed up because you did not feel you were good enough.

The more worthy you feel, and the more accepting you are of yourself, the more ready you are to receive.

The last time someone gave you a compliment, did you say thank you or did you go into a million reasons why it wasn't justified? If you cannot receive something as simple as a compliment, how ready are you to receive your vision?

Start forming the habit of receiving graciously. Accept things that come your way. If you begin to dismiss them, take a close look at why you are acting this way. Is it a past way of thinking? Are you feeling unworthy and talking yourself out of receiving it? Learn to thank people, situations and the universe for sending you everything that comes your way. Practice the art of being grateful for everything given to you.

A lot of people have opportunities right at their door but do not realize it. They are waiting for something to happen to allow them to take the opportunity, or for someone to hand it to them. There are people right now looking for jobs but continuing to collect unemployment insurance. Their friends have relatives who own businesses or have opportunities for them but for whatever reason, they do not feel worthy enough to apply for a job. They are waiting for the friend to ask the relative to call them. Take a look around at what situation you are currently in. Is there an opportunity right in front of you now that could take you one step closer to your vision? If so, why aren't you acting on it? Don't wait for others to come to you, learn to go to them. You are worth it.

Along with receiving you need to keep the energy moving with giving. The law of perpetual motion guarantees that the energy you are sending out has to be returned to you. If you want to receive something really big all you have to do is send out some powerful energy. Whatever energy you send out it has to be replenished.

The energy has to flow through you. Send weak energy and you will get weak results. Send strong energy, get strong results.

You may have the vision that you are the lead guitarist in a band. You currently own a guitar, have the music books, but do not know how to play. If you do not put time and energy into learning how to play, practicing regularly, and spending your time focusing on your plan, chances are you will not reach your goal. The more energy you put into the dream of being a guitarist the better chance you have of opportunities coming your way. Your time and effort has to be so focused that you spend as much energy as you can on learning to play the guitar. The more you put in, the better your results.

When you focus on your vision with clarity, you will begin to see the energy coming back to you in different ways. Your instructor may see your improvement and recommend you to play at an event or help another student. The opportunities will start presenting themselves to you and you need to see them as stepping stones towards your goal. If you block the chances and refuse to give service, you are blocking the energy. When you find yourself giving and receiving on a regular basis, and it is mainly doing what you love, your days will be so fulfilling. And if you can eventually be paid to do it, you will love going to work each and every day.

When you understand this concept you will learn to keep the flow going and expect the results. Your energy flow will get easier, faster, harder and stronger. You will grow as a person and get amazing results. The energy flow cannot be blocked at any time. It needs to be in a constant state of passing through you. For it to be continuous, it is just as important to receive as it is to give. If you block the passing of energy it will cause a negative reaction.

What happens when you give all your energy to something and you reap all the rewards, but then you stop giving back? How many times have you heard about someone working their way to the top only to find when they get there, they forget everyone and everything that helped them get there.

This is no different than the actor who starts off working as a waiter, living in deplorable conditions, doing anything and everything to survive just so he can devote his free time to study to be an actor. They rely on others to help them when they don't have enough money or friends for moral support.

They eventually get a break and land a role in a part that makes them famous. They shoot to the top and suddenly their fans are paying to see them in every film they make. The actor becomes super rich and buys all the luxuries in life that they always dreamed about. The fans are just as responsible for his success as he is. Without them he would be nothing. But then we hear about them being seen on the street or at an event where an excited fan asked for an autograph and the star refused. These individuals may then become overpowering and totally unbearable to work with. They become known as the "Diva" on the set. In the end no one hires them because of their attitude and they go off into obscurity.

What service will you be providing or giving? Think about the things you can give to others to create a positive flow of energy.

When we give to others there is that wonderful feeling we get, that warm and fuzzy emotion of seeing someone happy. That vibration you feel is positive energy created inside of you. It is a wonderful feeling. Ask any philanthropist who donates their time or money to a charity about the way they feel after their contributions. Many of these individuals have worked hard to achieve their goals and in return share it with those that are in need. They are grateful for their receipt of abundance and are ready to keep the flow in motion.

It is like a house that is extremely warm on a summer day. To cool down the house you need to cause a breeze, but if you only open the front window the air cannot flow. You are receiving the outside air but it cannot breeze through the house. In order for it to flow you need to open the back window. By opening both windows the air can pass through and it cools the home.

To keep the flow of your energy, you must open the door to receiving, but also open the door to giving. The more time and energy you spend giving and working towards your goal, the more you will get back in the form of results.

CHAPTER 20

The Movie Trailer

A movie studio focuses all their energy on the completion of a movie so they may distribute it to the public. The goal is to attract a paying audience so they can make back not only what it cost to produce the movie but some profit as well.

As their movie was created in a controlled location, the studio now needs to release it to its intended audience to start the ball rolling. They need to find their target market and entice them to come and see their movie.

The studios do this by creating a trailer of the movie to attract their intended demographic. This trailer is a highlight reel showing some of the best shots in the movie and it includes all the messages necessary to evoke interest from the public. It is an advertisement shown in theatres, on television and the Internet to attract as many viewers as possible.

The studios know the power of repetition, so the more they show the trailer, the more people see it and will go to the movie.

Studios do a lot of research first, to find out who their intended audience is, where to advertise, then how many times they need to show their trailer in front of those people to attract them to their product.

You began this journey by creating your own movie studio and you spent a lot of energy working on your production, thinking about and envisioning every detail. You worked your imagination until you got your final vision and hopefully, you have a clear goal of what you want to achieve. You came up with an idea and now you need to attract what you need for the results to happen. The good news is that you are not focusing on attracting a certain demographic.

You are focusing on attracting only one customer . . . the Universe. It is your customer and it will deliver to you exactly what you advertise.

You have been working on developing your idea, clarifying every detail of what you wanted to attract, and you should have a clear understanding of the process of how it will come to you. You have been working on your trailer and your message should be getting clear. Now you need to make a highlight reel of your vision, one that has the best shots of you. This trailer needs to depict who you want to become, what you are doing and what you have accomplished. It is your final result. This is your vision trailer.

Like the studio, you need to know that the more you project it, the more energy you will attract. You need to have the projector, your subconscious mind and run this trailer continuously day and night.

When you wake up in the morning, go to bed at night, or any time in between, watch your trailer. Project it as many times a day that you can. Just like the movie studios, repetition is the key to getting the audience to remember it.

You are working to clear the reruns that were in your subconscious mind for a long time. You need to review and keep this new movie in your mind as often as possible.

It is the repetition of this movie that is going to erase the old reruns. You must run this trailer in your mind over and over again until it runs without you thinking about it. It will become your habit and eventually you will become the trailer.

When you sync up all of your senses with the vision that you want, you will put in motion a series of events that will attract everything that you want.

The universe will send back to you exactly what you project in your mind. Watch your new trailer continuously and get excited about it. Know that it is in production and going to be shown. The more strongly you feel about something, the more passionate you will be, and this will allow you to see and accept more things into your life, that you may never have in the past. When you know who you are and what you want, you will see it more clearly.

The belief that you have in yourself should be so strong and so clear, that everything you are creating is from the inside. It will start flowing from you outwards and it will allow you to see what you need to make your vision come to fruition. It is just like attracting your demographic. You know who you are advertising to, so you know when it comes to you to allow it in.

This is what my son did with his Ninja Turtle movie. He had run that movie in his mind so many times, over and over again, from the moment he woke up until he went to sleep. Eventually, he believed he was a ninja turtle, and that he was a hero fighting crime. The signs of this characteristic did not stop there. This movie resonated with something that he had inside of himself naturally. His character was to serve and protect. I saw this come through in other areas in his life as he was growing up, but none as obvious as the person he is today as he serves in the Canadian Armed Forces.

When you are operating from your true nature and you are being your true self, you are more powerful and it is more liberating. You are creating a new movie that no one has seen before, and it is one of a kind, so don't be surprised if people line up to see it. You are making this movie to release your natural passion which is being starved and needs to be nourished and grown.

There have been many movies in the past that were done for reasons other than making money. They were done because someone believed in the message so much that their passion was to just get it done. Sometimes, the movie becomes a hit and makes millions of dollars in revenue and has results that no one expected. This type of movie is called a sleeper. It was a seed that lay dormant, was awakened, was brought to life and nurtured, and turned into a blockbuster hit.

You have had this seed inside you all this time, just waiting for you to awaken and nurture it. Your Sleeper is ready to be released.

CHAPTER 21

The Final Production

I think it's only fair at this point to give you a couple of scripts that I feel would outline what the process looks like from start to finish. Firstly, how being stuck with our old movie can take control of our lives without us knowing and keep us from growing as individuals and in turn, cause us to disintegrate. Secondly, how to keep a vision and how controlling our thoughts help our dreams come to fruition.

I want to first review Thelma and Louise. I think this is one of the best scripts that show how an individual can be stuck in circumstances, living in conditions they are not happy with, but learn to accept it. When we do not become our true selves naturally and we are forced to suppress, it is released negatively and this script is a perfect example.

Thelma is played by Geena Davis. She is a beautiful, outgoing person, living in a home with a verbally abusive, controlling husband, who does not show her any love or respect. Her outlet is her friend, Louise, played by Susan Sarandon, who is a waitress in a diner, has a boyfriend, but most of all, has a Ford Thunderbird convertible. The movie is based on the women having the opportunity to venture away to a cabin for the weekend, away from life's worries. Unfortunately, their weekend, while being adventurous, has a more negative outcome.

Both of these women have not been living to their true potential, have been suppressing their anger and resentment (mostly towards men) and are thrust into a series of events that slowly exposes their past for us to see.

Thelma, who is used to being controlled by a man, finds herself in a situation where a man at a roadhouse bar tries to rape her. Louise, who we can assume by dialogue throughout the movie was once raped herself, finds Thelma in the parking lot being raped, chooses not to call for help from the patrons or the police, but takes the law into her own hands and shoots the man dead.

Both women are reacting to what they know, what the rerun has been playing in their subconscious minds, even though they know it is wrong and not what they want. Thelma wants a man to respect and love her but she attracts a man even worse than her husband. Louise, obviously reacting to her own experience, is convinced that when you get raped you are blamed for it, and believes you have to take care of yourself. Both were operating from past reruns.

As the movie goes on, we find Thelma being subjected to new experiences, which in turn awaken emotions in her she never felt before. Unfortunately, most of the actions were negative and she continued to attract bad men with bad results. Louise on the other hand, continued to push away the good that comes to her, never learning to trust, even when it was in her best interest.

As these characters prove in the movie, if we do not focus on growth we will go into disintegration. When we do not feed what is positive, the negative will come through and take over. As the movie goes on the women not only accept that they are now criminals, they begin to believe they are criminals, and become even more reckless and dangerous. They continue to feed this new belief until it transforms them into outlaws.

In the end, the belief that these women had in men, in the justice system, mixed with their low self-esteem, created a formula so destructive that the only way they saw out was to end their lives. They saw no future, had no hope, and therefore ended their suffering.

Thelma and Louise is one of my favorite movies with a brilliant story line and a true example to me of what can happen when we do not take control of our thinking. Your mind will always feed your way of thinking, whether it is positive or negative.

If I had to choose one movie that from start to finish depicted what I have asked of you in this book, one movie that outlined every step of obtaining the goal you want in life, it would have to be The Shawshank Redemption. This was a film created from a book by Steven King.

The movie shows us that, when you have full control of what you have inside your mind, even when your external self is being controlled by someone physically, they cannot take what you have internally. And it is that part that creates your results.

The story revolves around Andy Dufresne, a successful banker who is sentenced to two life terms for the murder of his wife and her lover.

Andy follows the steps of creating a vision in his mind and keeping it there no matter what the circumstances. During his time in prison he is subjected to continuous unimaginable abuse. However, throughout his incarceration, he remains true to his vision. He knows he is innocent and always believes that one day he will be free. He is so precise with his goal that he not only dreams of freedom, he sees himself on the beaches of Zihuatanejo, Mexico, sanding and rebuilding an old boat. This is a tall order for someone who is in jail for life.

One thing Andy does throughout the movie is keep his vision to himself. He never reveals his plan for freedom to anyone. He continues to work it throughout the entire movie, without input from others. He keeps it alive in his mind no matter what happens around him.

Andy is a persistent man and this character shows through in everything he does. If he wants something he goes after it, no matter how long it takes. He knows that if he does things methodically and in detail he will get results. This is shown to us with his rock carving and his acquiring a library for the prison, obtained by writing letters once a week for six years. When he wants something he goes after it no matter the circumstances.

An example of how Andy keeps his energy flowing, even in prison is that when Andy gets rewarded for anything, he shares his gifts with the other inmates.

The power of music and how it inspires is also noted in this movie. In the new shipment of books for the library, there is a record of an opera that he loves. You could see the care and the love he has for this music by the way he handles the record before he plays it. It awakens in him something he hadn't felt in a very long time. It inspires him and he in turn, allows the rest of the inmates to share in the music. This gesture gets him thrown in solitary confinement but it was the music that he held in his mind that got him through the two weeks in solitary. He keeps the music alive inside him and it is the power of his mind that keeps him motivated towards his goal.

Andy shows the power of his will several times throughout the movie. The prison may have control of Andy physically, but not of his mind. He is free to keep his hopes, dreams and visions alive throughout his incarceration.

The recurring message through the movie is "get busy living or get busy dying." This is the message to you as a creative being to remember that you must constantly be growing; if not, you will disintegrate. Your vision needs to be nourished and allowed to grow.

Andy was always creating new opportunities and making changes and as he grew, other characters were affected by him and his energy. He may have had resistance but he always stayed true to what he believed in. Eventually those around him began to believe in him as he made things happen. He knew how to stand up for what he believed in and did whatever it took to make it come about.

In the end we discover Andy's main secret, his true vision, to be a free man. It is revealed that he had been tunneling through his cell walls for the past 19 years, bit by bit, with persistence and detail he constructed a plan that not only frees him from prison, but leaves him with a comfortable amount of money to live on. The movie ends with him sanding his boat on the beaches of Mexico, being greeted by his recently paroled friend, Red.

Andy always kept his vision alive, no matter what the circumstance. He used his imagination and his will to get the results he wanted.

I have a lot of hope like Andy that you discovered how to use your imagination in a productive way to help you achieve your goals and keep your vision alive. You have your own ideas, your own thoughts, and only you can nurture them. Know that you are the only one who needs to see it to make it happen.

I hope you are sparked to see a movie and look at it a little differently than you may have in the past. Perhaps there will be a character that you resonate with that reminds you that anything is possible. Take notice of the many details that it takes to put a movie into production and know that if you spend time on the details you too can produce great results.

Before a script is ever produced, the production company sees the finished product in their minds and believes it's worth putting all their time and energy into making it. Imagine how many sensational individuals there would be in this world, if we all took the time and effort to script our lives and produce them the same way a movie studio does.

CUT

PRINT

Acknowledgements

Lost in Translation, *2003, Focus Features*
Teenage Mutant Ninja Turtles, *1987 TV. CBS, 1990, Golden Harvest, Limelight Entertainment, 888 Productions, Mirage Enterprises, Northshore Investments*
Rocky, *1976, Chartoff-Winkler Productions, United Artists*
Overboard, *1987, Metro-Goldwyn Mayer, Hawn/Sylbert Movie Company, Star Partners*
Mother, *1996 Paramount Pictures, Scott Rudin Productions,*
Wizard of Oz, *1939, Metro-Goldwyn-Mayer*
Big, *1988, Twentieth Century Fox, Gracie Films*
Star Wars, *1977, Lucasfilm, Twentieth Century Fox*
Raiders of the Lost Ark, *1981, Paramount Pictures, Lucasfilm*
Ace Ventura Pet Detective, *1994, Morgan Creek Productions*
Roxanne, *1987, Columbia Pictures*
Chaplin, *1992, Carolco Pictures*
Horrible Bosses, *2011, New Line Cinema*
The Way We Were, *1973, Columbia Pictures Corporation*
Field of Dreams, *1989, Gordon Company, Universal Pictures*
Paradise, *1991, Touchstone Pictures*
Grease, *1978, Paramount Pictures*
Hook, *1991, Amblin Entertainment, TriStar Pictures*
Thelma and Louise, *1991, Pathe Entertainment, Metro-Goldwyn-Mayer*
Shawshank Redemption, *1994, Castle Rock Entertainment*

Francesca Banting resides in Vancouver, British Columbia and is founder of Dreampath Consulting.

Contact information:

www.dreampath.ca

info@dreampath.ca

YOUR LIFE AS A MOVIE
Scripting and Producing Your Dreams Into Reality

www.yourlifeasamovie.ca

167

52881376R00100

Made in the USA
San Bernardino, CA
01 September 2017